<u>Poems by Paige</u>

Poems about love, feeling emotions, finding strength and uplifting inspiration

Author - Alisa Paige

Introduction

This is My Passion Poem

This is my passion,
Beyond any fashion,
They're stories I tell,
Describing all of us so well,
Not a quote that doesn't rhyme,
But a feeling we've all felt many times,
I love to express what's in my heart and soul,
Sharing and helping others, gives me a warm, happy glow.

Poems by Paige, poems to help flow through every aspect of life

Poetry Book Description

A collection of over 100 heartfelt poems I wrote to help soothe, inspire and celebrate all that we, as living beings, go through, can relate to, and that pertain to all aspects and emotional feelings in life. I hope you enjoy them as much as I enjoy writing them, expressing within them and sharing them. Peace and love and let things flow.

Book Dedication

This book is dedicated to my Kyle, Todd, mshbmil, my sweet puppies and to all my loved ones, here and in Heaven, and I know you're always with me. You all inspire me to be a better person, encourage me, support me in all things that I do and I'm so thankful and grateful for you all staying by my side. And a special thank you to God. Thank you and I love you all!

Chapter 1
<u>Love and Friendship</u>

Chapter 2
<u>Love and Loss</u>

Chapter 3
Emotions, Feelings and Coping

Chapter 4
Strength, Courage and Healing

Chapter 5
<u>Inspirational and Uplifting</u>

Chapter 1

<u>Love and Friendship</u>

My Dream Poem, like a Cinderella Fantasy

Long ago and far away,
I dreamt of you, to come my way,
When I first saw you, your smile so sweet,
I knew right then, we were meant to meet,
How I've dreamt of you Prince Charming, to freely come to me,
The look in your eyes, told me it was meant to be,
The smile on your face, was priceless and precious,
I knew then, it was only you, from here on, I'd want kisses,
I never thought I'd meet you, you're so far from real,
But what I felt in my heart, I never thought I'd feel,
The pull from your smile, I could look at you all day,
If you asked, I'd follow, wherever you want, in any way,
In my dreams you've always been, in my dreams you'll always stay,
But I'll never stop dreaming, of being with you someday,
It's a shame that dreams sometimes, are better than reality,
In my dreams, you're mine, and for now, that's where I'll leave it be.

-by Paige

You Stole My Heart Poem

When I wasn't even looking,
You came along,
You stole my heart,
Just like in a song,

You gave me hope,
That love exists,
The true, deep love,
That never quits,

The kind we dream of,
It keeps on going,
More beautiful every day,
It keeps on growing,

I've heard it can be real,
But never quite believed,
I wished I'd find it too,
But now it can be perceived,

You taught me that,
The true meaning of love,
I'm so lucky to have you,
You were sent from up above,

I can't imagine life without you,
Since you came into my life,
Forever in my heart and soul,
You took away all strife,

You have my heart always,
Now and for all eternity,
The love I only imagined,
To find and have, to be that lucky,

I'm blessed beyond measure,
You, forever hold the key,
To my heart, my love, my being,
You stole it and were meant for me.

-by Paige

Growing Old Together Poem

Sometimes things aren't perfect,
It's a roller coaster ride,
Going up and down,
Jerking from side to side,

Sometimes slow and rolling,
Sometimes fast with screams,
But during the whole time,
Together, we're a team,

What starts out as fresh,
New and all butterflies,
Turns into comfort,
Every night, next to each other we lie,

It can be more than hard at times,
But also fun and laughs,
Going through the motions,
Some things are hard to grasp,

The fun times are so special,
Knowing you're on each other's side,
That there's someone always with you,
Everywhere, along for the ride,

But then you may hit a bump,
The hard times are there too,
Even when you're not ready,
They come from out of the blue,

It's really hard to make it,
To stay and see it through,
From fighting, lies, maybe betrayal,
Everything rosy can turn blue,

But if you truly love each other,
Deep down in your heart,
You make it through somehow,
Can't imagine being apart,

When you see that you're there,
Helping each other through hardships,
It makes you realize no one's perfect,
But somehow, you just fit,

The ease when things are good,
It's so nice to just have,
To know you're not alone,
Makes you so grateful and glad,

Putting up with the annoyances,
We all have them you know,
But if you love someone enough,
Weigh pros and cons, and let them go,

Love isn't always easy,
Life isn't like a romantic movie,
But with faith, trust and forgiveness,
It's love, how at its finest, can be,

When life has its rough patches,
It's nice to have that bond,
Knowing you can count on each other,
Growing old together and staying strong.

-by Paige

The Laughter that We've Shared Poem

The laughter that we've shared,
Has always proved we cared,
The times when we were down,
Near each other we were always around,
I don't know what I'd do without you,
You're the one I know to be genuine and true,
Through the years we've just grown fonder,
Because with you I'll never have to wonder,
What it's like to have a best friend,
Soulmates with no end,
You bring me smiles and happiness,
To me, you'll always be a notch above the rest.

-by Paige

To My Love, Sent From Heaven Above Poem

To my love,
Sent from Heaven above,
I always waited for you,
And now my dreams have come true,
You were brought straight to me,
You and I were meant to be,
To never be apart,
Forever in my heart,
I'm so glad that I was patient,
While others came and went,
I knew that they weren't right,
I had only you in my sight,
Now that we're together,
We make each other better,
We'll never drift apart,
For you love, are my heart.

-by Paige

You to Me, Well You are the Best Poem

To the ocean breeze,
To the falling leaves,
To the cozy nights, and blooms in the spring,
To the ends of the Earth,
To the last and the first,
To the moon, beach and back, you make my heart sing,

To the shore and to the hills,
To the mountains and to the mills,
Through the rain, the snow and the slush,
You'll always be my favorite thing,
With the pure happiness you bring,
Forever on you I'll always have a crush,

You make my heart happy,
You make me smile with glee,
Safely tucked away, within me you'll stay,
In everything I do,
It's all about you,
You're my first and last thought of each day,

I can't imagine what life would be,
Had you not been given to me,
I'll forever be grateful and blessed,
For with you I can be me,
See everything more clearly,
You to me, well you are the best.

-by Paige

You'll Always Be My Favorite Poem

From the moment I saw you and held you in my arms,
I knew you were going to be my greatest of lucky charms,
Watching you sleep, and grow, taking note of every breath,
Made me finally realize, that true love has no depth,
Protecting you and guiding you, I hope I did it well,
Looking at the person you've become, with proudness I can tell,
I did my job, but to me it never felt like work,
I just always want the best for you, and that you'll never be hurt,
So in my arms, still getting hugs, and always in my heart,
You've always been a blessing, we'll never be far apart,
For in my soul, you'll always be my favorite and number one,
No matter where, no matter how, beneath, above the moon and the sun.

-by Paige

You Were Made to Be Mine Poem

You've always been there for me morning, day and night,
When I didn't want to get out of bed, or if I woke up out of fright,
You took care to always be there, no matter the circumstance,
You're the one I always counted on, never not by my side, never, not a chance,
In my heart you'll always stay, forever, for all eternity,
Whether we're near or whether we're apart, together we'll always be,
It doesn't matter where, it doesn't matter what time,
Forever I'll be grateful, that you were made to be mine.

-by Paige

You Saved Me Poem

You are my love,
My radiant sunshine from above,
You taught me life, and to love,
And how to rise above,
Without you I would be nothing,
Weak, no future hopes and roughing,
Because of you I know loving,
Nothing in the world could ever be above it,
You in your angelic love saved me,
You'll never know, but you braved me,
I didn't know, but I was caving,
And you I'll never be trading,
I don't know what I'd do without you,
You're the one I needed and never knew,
I can never show you all my gratitude,
But you're the one love, that keeps me sane and true.

-by Paige

The Love Fantasy Poem

It's like I've always loved you,
But it wasn't meant to be,
It is better in my mind though,
The perfect love fantasy,

We think it's supposed to be perfect,
We want the ultimate love,
That we think everyone else has,
Fitting together, like a glove,

But nothing ever is,
And no relationship ever will,
Be perfect in every way,
And your every wish fulfilled,

People may make it seem,
Like it's perfection all the time,
But that's just not real life,
Beyond any reason or rhyme,

No problems do they face,
They're happy and never quarrel,
Never get on each other's nerves,
Never come upon any sorrow,

Unfortunately that's not the case,
No matter what they say,
They may just not show it,
Or may let go and start new each day,

I'd rather keep it a fantasy,
So perfect in my dreams,
Nothing ever goes wrong,
With us, it's perfect it seems,

I don't ever want it ruined,
Or stained with any dismay,
Or not turning out the way I want,
And have dreamt of to this day,

Forever it will always last,
Wrapped tight in each other arms,
Never wanting for anyone else,
Never tiring of each other's charms,

Always seeing each other,
Through rose colored glasses,
Never losing our attraction,
No matter how much time passes,

Staying faithfully in love,
And never wanting to let go,
Feeling close in every possible way,
Our love only passionately grows,

For some it may, some it might not,
But for me, every night we remain,
In my beautiful, sweet, perfect dreams,
Constantly our love is the same,

Nothing can touch it, it's all that I want,
I can make it different and still,
Every dream of us is good and better,
Than any realistic love could feel,

We all want the perfect love,
Where nothing ever goes wrong,
Only in fantasies, and in our dreams,
Can our life be a perfect love song,

Because there's no such thing on Earth,
For anyone, with you or with me,
Only a love fantasy, we all wish for,
That stays perfect, so dream, and let it be.

-by Paige

I'm so in Love with You Poem

I'm so in love with you,
No one else will do,
No one can compare,
To the feelings that I bare,
You're what I always dreamed of,
What everyone wants from love,
The simple love from above,
But that's what dreams are made of,
Will dreams they always be?
Between both you and me?
I really don't care,
What anyone has to share,
They can say whatever they want,
Continue to tease and taunt,
But that doesn't change my mind,
When I dream of true love I find,
You're the only one for me,
If only everyone could see,
We belong together,
Now, and always forever,
Will it always be this way?
Forever in our hearts we'll stay?
Together and forever true,
I'll always belong to you,
No one can step in our way,
No one can make us betray,
Each other's love we feel,
We were given, so very real,
And never would I want to,
Be with anyone but you.

-by Paige

I Want a Love Poem

I want a love,
That secretly grows,
Beyond any reason,
For reasons nobody knows,

That lasts day to day,
Through so much turmoil,
And at the end of the day,
All problems are foiled,

The love that lasts,
Through thick and thin,
If bad things arise,
It can renew again,

Nothing gets past it,
Years, pain or age,
No matter what we go through,
We always engage,

In each other's feelings,
In each other's lives,
It's how we remain stable,
In each other's eyes,

Time won't change it,
The feelings we knew,
Above all else,
Our feelings just grew,

Isn't it what we all want?
And secretly wish for?
Someone we can count on,
Forever more,

Why can't we all have that?
Where is our true love fate?
How do we search?
Where do we trace?

The path that is uncertain,
That none of us knows,
We can only imagine,
What time will show,

But we keep on searching,
And we keep believing,
That we'll get lucky someday,
Just like everyone is craving,

I hope I find the one,
And I hope that they find me,
So we can together see,
What we, and love, are meant to be.

-by Paige

True Friends are Gems Poem

What we all want,
Are honest, true friends,
The ones that are genuine,
Are rare, precious gems,

Always on your side,
No matter what,
You can count on them,
And you have the same thoughts,

So much alike,
And so much the same,
Different very little,
Some only by name,

No matter how far away,
The friendship just lasts,
Through all of life's changes,
No matter how many years pass,

It's like nothing has changed,
When you see each other again,
So much to talk about,
No one has to pretend,

Because you're always in touch,
Wherever you are,
It's like you're not really apart,
Distance is never far,

You know everything,
About one another,
Every little secret,
Like no other,

And you wouldn't share them,
Your secrets are safe,
Just like you are together,
Your ground no one can shake,

For it's true and solid,
The bond never-ending,
It's the special ones you keep,
Together forever blending,

You may not have known,
Before you even met,
That they would be the friends,
You forever kept,

They're ones that are solid,
That special bond,
That only gets better,
It was, and always will be strong,

Like time won't change,
The love and loyalty,
You have for each other,
Inside, it will always be,

Always in each other's corner,
Each other you'd always defend,
Yes those are the friends we all want,
True friends, are gems, with no end.

-by Paige

You Weren't a Mistake Poem

You weren't a mistake,
Any blame I take,
I couldn't even imagine,
Or start to ever fathom,
A life without you,
It's like nothing I ever knew,
The love that you give,
Is for all that I live,
It means more to me,
Than anything could ever be,
Bigger than the sky,
Or an eagle flying by,
More powerful,
Than any rivers flow,
Stronger than any sea,
Is your love to me,
The love from you I take,
I never would forsake,
No line could ever trace,
Nothing could replace,
The depths to which,
You've reached and kept,
The love of my heart and soul,
With you it's only grown,
And it forever will,
Even if time stands still,
For you and I,
There is no end time,
Our love will forever stay,
We are each other's way.

-by Paige

Neither of Us Was Searching Poem

What am I doing?
I've fallen for a stranger,
I didn't mean to,
It could be a life changer,

Neither of us was searching,
Or even looking for someone,
Then one day it hit us,
It started as just fun,

There's something about him,
It feels so natural,
Talking every day,
He always texts and calls,

First thing in the morning,
And before I go to bed,
All during the day,
I can't get him out of my head,

Funny thing is,
We haven't even met,
In person that is,
Just not yet,

We're planning it though,
To know if it's real,
We're both being cautious,
We can tell how we feel,

Neither of us is naive,
But it's going so fast,
We want to make sure,
It's going to last,

How can you fall for someone,
So fast and so quick?
We know all about each other,
What makes each other tick,

The words he uses,
And what he says to me,
Have me flying high,
Everyone can see,

My happiness shows,
But will it last?
Do fairytales exist?
It's like a love spell was cast,

Upon each of us,
And we both agree,
We have finally found,
Our missing puzzle piece,

If it doesn't work out,
When we finally meet,
I hope we can stay friends,
To me, he's such a treat,

I'm hoping, but scared,
That it will all work out,
Because finding a love like this,
Is what we all dream about.

-by Paige

Sunshine After the Rain Poem

You've taken away my stress,
You've taken away my pain,
You've made me feel happy,
Like sunshine after the rain,

You lifted my spirits,
That were flying so low,
To feel this glowing high,
Is something I didn't know,

You repaved the way,
Made me change course,
For my new, sweet path,
But nothing was forced,

You've shown me new ways,
That sweet words can be spoken,
I feel like Sleeping Beauty,
Has finally awoken,

I had a comfortable life,
On the straight and narrow,
Then you came along,
And shot me with Cupid's arrow,

I never knew feelings,
Could be shown so sincere,
In hard for me in words,
But in my poetry it's clear,

It amazes and blows my mind,
The things you say to me,
How the romance just flows,
And comes so naturally,

I wish I had that trait,
To express out loud my emotions,
But we're all different we know,
Maybe there's different love potions,

That help us to show,
What we feel inside,
But when you're truly, deeply happy,
That's something you can't hide,

I can't hide it at least,
It glows from the inside out,
And hopefully shows my true feelings,
And what I'm all about,

No one has to guess,
What's going on inside of me,
Love has a way of showing,
With no doubt if you believe,

Believe you deserve it,
And believe it will come,
When you least expect it,
Like for me, you may be the one.

-by Paige

Thought We Were Over Poem

I thought we were over,
All said and done,
I thought you'd be happy,
You'd be ready to run,

You'd wanted to for so long,
Always mentioned it freely,
Maybe we should get a divorce,
Every time hard to deal with,

You had your wild times,
A midlife crisis they say,
I stayed with you through it,
Wasn't easy, but found a way,

I felt unappreciated,
Unloved and unwanted,
When empty nest happened,
I'd let you go flaunt it,

You wanted out,
And I did too,
But for a long time,
I remained true,

Then it happened,
I found someone else,
Not for a lifetime,
Just something for myself,

That ended, which is fine,
But then I felt it again,
That spark and excitement,
When fun and romance begin,

So not even looking,
Someone else came along,
All in perfect timing,
It was beautiful like a song,

This one you found out about,
I didn't hide it so well,
I didn't care to though,
And I knew you could tell,

Then it was me who said it,
Let's separate,
I've found another,
For us, I thought it was too late,

I thought you'd be elated,
Finally set free,
Empty nest was happening,
And you didn't need or want me,

But once the tables were turned,
You saw how much it hurts,
You actually cried and realized,
Emotional cuts are worse,

They stab into your heart,
Cut you to the bone,
Hurt your very soul,
You feel so sick and alone,

I'd never made you feel that,
Even though I had,
I didn't want to hurt you,
I honestly thought you'd be glad,

But another side came out,
Something you hadn't shown,
The part of you that deeply loved me,
A part I hadn't known,

I don't think you knew it either,
We weren't happy and were over,
But it actually made you see me,
And like a lucky four leaf clover,

It appeared and it showed,
The love inside you felt,
It took me awhile to reciprocate,
But then you made my heart melt,

Seeing this side of you,
Learning you didn't want to let me go,
I guess it took someone else coming in,
To make you see my glow,

It's been a rough time,
But if this is what it took to fix,
Our marriage and relationship,
I wouldn't change the mix,

Because like mixing a recipe,
It brought us back together,
We both finally realize,
We love and want each other forever.

-by Paige

The One I Never Knew Poem

I always had an attraction to you,
Even though we never met,
I wanted to meet you so much,
But why, I hadn't known yet,

You would be the one,
I pour my heart out to,
The one I always dreamt of,
The one I never knew,

Something deep inside of me,
Felt drawn to you somehow,
To a person I didn't know,
But felt an energy about,

It would be years before we met,
But once we did we knew,
All along we were meant to be,
Between so far and so few,

In each other's lives,
We didn't even know we missed,
Each other's love so sweet,
Until our hearts felt kissed,

With each other's love,
That we'd both needed for so long,
You were always in my heart,
And in my life, all along.

-by Paige

You'll Know the Loyal Ones Poem

Many times it seems,
We have ones who care,
In all of the good times,
That are always there,

But it's in those others,
The times when we despair,
We find out the true ones,
The love that will stay there,

Sometimes we can't see past,
Or we may not recognize,
The loyalty some seem to show,
But then ignore our cries,

It's just that, they aren't loyal,
Of a love that we need,
We thought we could trust,
Beside us they'd always be,

Thankfully there are ones,
That are loyal beyond measure,
They show who they are,
And they're who we need to treasure,

They're there in good times,
And in hard times they stay,
Right by our side,
To help from day to day,

Their caring and their love,
They make to us shown,
So we don't have to wonder,
If we'll ever be alone,

Figure out and keep those ones,
Never let them go,
Show you'd do the same for them,
The bond you have will grow,

When it comes right down to it,
And everyone else runs,
You'll see the ones that stay,
You'll know the loyal ones.

-by Paige

A True Friendship Poem

When I first met you, that very first day,
I knew we were going to click, I knew right away,
We talked and we laughed, we became friends so fast,
A friendship that's real, that grows and will last,
You're my friend, my confidant, you hold the key to my secrets,
You understand the reasoning I have no regrets,
I can talk to you about anything, you never judge my ways,
You've helped through rough times, to see better days,
Whether it be my health or love, even helping me walk,
If I fall, I know with you I'll always be caught,
You're there for me, completely, whatever my woe,
You comfort me and listen, a true friendship you show,
You've stayed by side, you show me you care,
Wanting a text when I'm safely home, forgetting, I wouldn't dare,
Friends like you don't come around too often,
Emotional and physical, the blows you help soften,
We come from the same place, maybe that's why we're in sync,
The way that we act, laugh, get along and think,
I hope that you know I'm there as much for you,
The friendship you've shown, is genuinely true,
You're always there for me, no matter day or night,
When I need to talk about what I'm doing, whether it be wrong or right,
I can talk to you about anything, nothing's off limits,
I hope you feel the same, no fakeness, no gimmicks,
With everything else you have going on,
With family, work or health, please know you are strong.
You get through tough times, and do so with spunk,
You can laugh through the pain, even when you're in a funk,
We can talk about serious issues at hand,
Then laugh about them in a way no one else could understand,
We're able to vent, to call each other names,
We know it's all in fun, in our laughter we have no shame,
We get it, the highs and lows of family and friends,
We can open up, talk serious, and laugh once again,
It's funny and all good because I know who you are,
You're my friend, and I love you, you're a beautiful bright, shining star,
I hope we're friends forever, I think we will be,
Not too much in life, do people understand each other so clearly,
You've put smiles on my face, more than you know,
I thank you so much for your love and concern that you always show,
You're always there for everyone, putting yourself last,
I want you to know you deserve love and happiness,
Pamper yourself more, and sometimes put yourself first,
You owe it to you, to be given the love you crave and thirst,
You're worth it you know, one of the best friends I have,
For being given our friendship, I'm more than just glad,

You're truly there in good times, in sickness and in health,
You and our friendship, are what really makes wealth,
And knowing you and me, with all we go through,
We'll get through it all, and shine through and through.

-by Paige

Realize the Ones Who are Really There Poem

Realize the ones who are really there,
For you, wherever you are, anywhere,
They're the ones you can always trust,
Your real, true loves that will never rust,
For these, certain beings in life,
That are never wrong, always right,
They're able to see outside your box,
And tell what lines you shouldn't cross,
Whether you listen, or you do not,
They won't leave you, never will taunt,
The way that they feel about you,
And know that you feel it too,
They know that you feel the same,
And, if there's any shame,
To how you are or what you're doing,
They'll still be there, no hellish hurrying,
You'll get there in your own time,
And be in the right frame of mind,
But until then,
They'll still be your friend,
Or your family,
Sadly, some of them can be the first to leave,
But the ones who stay and never go,
Are family, some blood, some not, no,
But always know who's there's for you,
No matter what, or what you've been through,
They are the ones to keep forever,
Through and through, never let go, not ever.

-by Paige

How'd I Get So Lucky Poem

How'd I get so lucky to find you?
Where you were before, I never knew,
I looked, and I had searched,
Far and wide upon this Earth,
At least I thought I had,
Until you showed up, I was sad,
Thinking there was no one,
That would be my certain someone,
My beautiful other half,
And one that's on my same path,
That thinks the way that I do,
And forever, our love would stay true,
No one coming between,
Any others, really can't be seen,
When you're in this much love,
It's sent from Heaven above,
Beyond our wildest dreams,
It's so unreal it seems,
To be this close to another,
And absolutely understand each other,
To feel yourself, and also be a pair,
For the same things, we both care,
It's hard to find when we're looking,
When you stop, that's when the flames start cooking,
For the one that's meant to be,
Forever, for you and me.

-by Paige

A True Love That's Really Mine Poem

Maybe someday I'll find,
A true love that's really mine,
That only I can hold onto,
And until the end, both be true to,
Does that really exist?
The dream with an endless kiss?
I want it to, and I wish,
For that beautiful bliss,
That only a certain seem to get,
For that love, we all seem to have wept,
Someday it'll be there,
And then, I'll be aware,
It's when we're not ready, that it shows up,
Into our lives, to fill our loving cup.

-by Paige

Animal Love Poem

The first time I saw you I knew,
We'd stick together like glue,
Our eyes met and fell in love,
You were sent from Heaven above,
I could see the fear in your eyes,
Your feelings had no disguise,
And mine knew from the start,
I needed new love in my heart,
Then they let us be together,
It was like birds of a feather,
We were meant to be and kismet,
Until then, we just hadn't met,
But maybe in our hearts we did,
For the loneliness we suddenly rid,
Our souls together felt a bond,
Something so real and so strong,
I couldn't leave without you,
It's something I just couldn't do,
The pull to me from you, has grown,
From something that was unknown,
Our love for each other has shown,
Maybe we didn't know we were prone,
To be together forever,
And apart, never ever,
The love of an animal is real,
They show exactly how they feel,
There's no mistaking or games,
We're able to help each other tame,
The restlessness inside,
That deep down we hide,
But when true loves meet,
With our hearts and souls, nothing can defeat,
Without even being able to speak,
Without words, we're able to peak,
To feel and show our true love,
That nothing could rise above,
There's no loyalty quite like an animal,
They are pure love, genuine and truthful.

-by Paige

Animals are Special Poem

Animals are special,
No matter what you say,
They're like no other being,
I wouldn't want it any other way,

They're there when you are happy,
Hugging and cuddling you,
They're there when you are sad,
Safe and lovingly holding you,

They're able to feel what's real,
That's all they ever show,
Never ever fake,
For that's all they know,

I even respect them more,
Than some of the people I've met,
Those people are the ones,
I want to try to forget,

Their meanness is real,
Fake beings it seems,
The bad people do exist,
Stay out of our lives and dreams,

For real our dreams are sweet,
Bad people are just nightmares,
Don't believe them for a second,
They're just there for scares,

Animals are different,
They show you face to face,
What they encumber,
And what you're about to embrace,

They show how they feel,
They don't fake it at all,
They give you the chance,
To fight and stand tall,

They don't keep you guessing,
Or pretend to be someone else,
They show who they are,
Never disguising themselves,

They may stalk and hunt,
But to live it's just their nature,
They don't mean any harm,
It's what they know and endure,

They don't know any different,
It's just love that they give,
They live to survive,
And survive how they live,

It's nature that's all,
They're so true blue,
You'll know if they surrender,
And give love to you,

Because they are bigger and wild,
And know no boundaries,
They fight for their life,
Or they know how to flee,

To go through what they must,
The hard times in their lives,
They're honest, brave and real,
They survive, love and thrive,

Whether it's love to their owner,
Or love to their young,
They're only trying to protect,
Themselves and their loved ones,

Love them in return,
And respect their needs,
They're just fighting for life,
It's their knowledge and their needs,

Don't ever hunt them though,
As you wouldn't want to be stalked,
And hunted by a predator,
That can't wait to grab you and taunt,

They are smarter than given credit,
They deserve much better too,
To be treated like a living being,
Because they are, just like me and you.

-by Paige

A Dogs Poem

If everyone were as loyal as dogs,
We could all be taught a lot,
Like how to love unconditionally,
Without anything artificially,
To be able to just relax and lay,
Or get the energy right then to play,
For we'd be up and awake,
Ready and able to take,
On anything,
The day will bring,
No snoozing alarm could keep us down,
When it's time, we'd be up and around,
Not deterred of any unknown noise,
Or afraid, no, we'd be poised,
If it shouldn't be there, we'll let it know,
It better hurry up and go,
Because we're not afraid,
Our territory is mapped out and laid,
Then we'll settle and retreat,
When those run off in defeat,
And lay down in delight,
And know we fought the fight,
Even if we didn't have to,
The enemy knows we will do,
Whatever it is that's needed,
And not end up depleted,
For we would always be ready,
No matter how heavy,
The day on us would bring,
Of each and everything,
Stretching is how we'd start our day,
Ready for whatever will come our way,
Or, to protect the ones we love,
And our homes and spaces in this world,
But in a second we can turn,
To be by the sides of the loves we yearn,
Hopefully they yearn for us too,
Because for all of our lives, we'll be true,
Waiting all day, till they get home,
It doesn't matter if we're alone,
We'll sleep, then be for them at the door,
Ready for hugs, food, treats and more,
Ready to play whenever they are,
When it's time to rest, we won't be far,
By their feet, we will be,
Ready for anything, awake or asleep,

When our tails wag, so hard and fast,
We knew deep down their absence wouldn't last,
From having to be gone, to pay our way,
Just a petting, rubbed belly, makes our day,
It lets us know, we were thought of too,
These rituals everyday, get us through,
And to be smothered in love,
With kisses and hugs,
We may only be parts of their world,
Next to them, on the bed, or on the couch curled,
If only for a small amount of time,
To dogs, their loved ones are their whole lives.

-by Paige

Chapter 2

<u>Love and Loss</u>

If Someone Lets You Go Poem

If someone lets you go,
It's much better to know,
Why be somewhere,
Where the other doesn't care?
You deserve much better,
Out of stormy weather,
Where there are brighter days,
And much happier ways,
Of being who you are,
And shining like a star,
Be around your tribe,
That has your same vibe,
So you feel a good fit,
And not misplaced a bit,
Be glad they let you go,
So you can thrive and grow,
And be loved as you are,
People will see from afar,
You and your new glow,
That wasn't able to show,
In a place not meant for you,
Where sadness only grew,
But now you can start fresh,
Start new and become your best,
Because being stifled can only,
Make you sad and lonely,
Once you see and feel great,
You won't again feel second rate,
You're the only YOU ever,
They'll never be one like you better,
You'll feel happier than before,
There's always another door,
To step into a new way of life,
No longer facing a knife,
That you didn't even know was there,
Being in it, you're not aware,
So be glad you're not still caught,
Now a new, happy life can be taught,
You're the greatest, now you know,
Go share your light, it'll show.

-by Paige

Just Believe Poem

It's sad when someone leaves,
But you have to believe,
If they're someone you love,
They're looking down from above,
Still with us and guiding us,
Believe and know this we must,
It's true and the only way,
To make it through each day,
They never leave our side,
They're with us along our ride,
Helping us by whispers,
In our ears only we can hear,
Don't ever think we're alone,
In lots of ways they've shown,
And continue to show and be,
With us in all of our needs,
Whether it be a butterfly,
Or a dragonfly flying by,
Or a ladybug appears,
Is how they show they are near,
But there are so many other things,
That they do and that they bring,
To let us know they're around,
Not far from us they can be found,
We so wish we could see them,
Touch, kiss and hug them again,
But if we listen with our hearts,
And be open, knowing we're not apart,
With our souls we can feel,
Them actually touching us for real,
And once again we'll be together,
Safely up in Heaven, forever.

-by Paige

My Love, Always By My Side Poem

My love for you will never fade,
I know you're still by my side,
You send me messages, I can't hear,
But able to hear with my mind,

You come into my dreams,
You save me from nightmares,
You hold me to dance,
Like we never had a care,

Like it never would end,
As all things seem to do,
But you show me you're still here,
I know, I can feel it's you,

You send me messages and signs,
You show me in so many ways,
If I just keep my eyes open,
I know you're still in all of my days,

You answer my questions, what you can,
When I ask them out loud or in my head,
Of things and moments from our past,
You speak to me from the dead,

It's amazing and comforting,
I can't even explain my smile,
When I know you've come to me,
And you heard me all the while,

When you can see in my head,
And you can see in my dreams,
And see in my day to day life,
The trouble life here brings,

Especially without you by my side,
Or able to reach you at any time,
It doesn't seem fair, taken away,
Without any reason or rhyme,

I can't just call you, so I scream your name,
And I hope that you will hear,
The pain and wanting and wishing,
That you can hurry to me and be near,

I feel lost most times without you,
But you show me you're at my side,
Whether I realize it or not,
You will always be my guide.

-by Paige

It's Hard to Let Someone Go Poem

It's hard to let someone go,
But inside we already know,
If they want to stay,
Oh the games we play,
When we first start out it's fun,
Something we haven't done,
In a really long time,
This closeness is hard to find,
Flirting as teens,
It's all new it seems,
You think you've grown close,
That they know you the most,
But then time will tell,
All too true and well,
You have to see and believe,
It never will be well received,
When hanging by a string,
And the bells really ring,
To cut the ties that bind,
You only have left in your mind,
Letting them go is hard,
They've moved on sweetheart,
Don't keep them as friends,
Or on social media where they pretend,
To still be your friend,
But never respond on their end,
You deserve better, that's a fact,
It's time to let go of lies, and that's that.

-by Paige

If You had Wanted to Stay Poem

If you had wanted to stay,
You would've,
If I wanted to make you stay,
I could've,
But I know now,
We're not meant to be,
It took awhile,
But I finally see,
It's still hard at times,
To get through a day,
Or go to sleep alone,
With no other way,
Of us staying together,
Why couldn't it last?
Make a future,
As fun as the past,
I don't know why,
It had to end,
But I do know now,
I need to mend,
To become whole,
And be fine by myself,
I knew it would happen,
Someday time would tell,
That for something,
And for some reason,
We were meant to have,
Only a season,
But that time I'll remember,
And so fondly of,
All that we shared,
The caring, the love,
It was meant for a time,
And that time I'll embrace,
Nothing takes it away,
Nothing can ever erase,
You will forever and always,
Live in my heart,
Even though we were meant,
To someday be apart,
I need to pick up,
The pieces left of me,
And try to move on,
Knowing another love will be.

-by Paige

Time to Walk Away Poem

We never know,
What's to come,
From the things we've said,
And the things we've done,

All the hurt,
All the pain,
Nothing helped,
And nothing gained,

It seems as if,
It's always the same,
Round and round,
We play the same game,

It doesn't seem to change,
Even though we want it to,
Some maybe don't,
But some maybe do,

Wish it could get better,
And be like it was,
Beautiful and easy,
Even when push came to shove,

We could say our peace,
What was on our minds,
Feelings might get hurt,
But would mend with time,

It seems as though lately,
That time has run out,
We can't even talk,
Without wanting to shout,

It's not healthy that way,
To always be upset,
Alone and misunderstood,
Not knowing what's next,

It's days, then weeks,
The months they fly,
Until we realize,
That now years have gone by,

We may speak occasionally,
But it's not easy now,
It's hard and uncomfortable,
The flow has gone south,

It's hard to get back,
To where we were before,
We always knew we could make up,
But now feels like the closing of a door,

And this time it's too hard to open,
The things being said behind,
To others about one another,
Peace and harmony is hard to find,

It's like the door is locked,
And no matter how hard one tries,
They can't get it open,
The key has been thrown aside,

So even if there's still love,
And a constant feeling of loss,
There's only so much to do,
To save it or sadly toss,

Keep trying if we can,
Or just set it free,
It will all work out,
The way it's supposed to be,

Whichever way,
Relief will be in sight,
Whether a reunion or a release,
Just know that we tried,

But we will deeply know,
Should we get to that day,
When we come to realize,
That it's time to walk away.

-by Paige

Missed Beyond Belief Poem

You're missed beyond belief,
I'll never get over the pain,
You helped me through everything,
My sunshine through the rain,

I could tell you anything,
You'd always understand,
You always had my back,
And always held my hand,

The hole that is inside of me,
Since you had to leave,
Though neither of us wanted you to,
Is too big to believe,

It will never be filled,
Nothing will ever replace,
Your love, your sincerity,
Your touch, the smile on your face,

Your laugh makes me smile,
Your hug brings me chills,
Of these sweet memories,
Nothing else can fulfill,

Although we try to find happiness,
In all walks of life,
You will always be irreplaceable,
For you, I'll always cry,

Tears of happiness, tears of joy,
Tears of missing you beyond,
What anyone could ever fathom,
For you, I'll always long,

You're always in my heart,
And always in my soul,
Always a part of me,
Everywhere I go,

I know you're always with me,
I feel you in so many ways,
You show it so deeply,
I wonder how hard it is to say,

The things to me, and things you do,
From beyond our life unknown,
But you are here, I know that's true,
I can see it in everything you've shown,

I don't know what it takes,
To come so openly to me,
I wish I could see and talk to you,
That's something I can't let be,

I always knew where you were,
We were always so in touch,
How could anyone so close,
Be ripped from someone's clutch?

So tight it's unbreakable,
When you have that deep, true love,
I guess that's just how it works,
On Earth and from Heaven above.

-by Paige

When a Song Comes On Poem

It's no mistake, the love we forsake, it never goes away,
No matter how hard we try, to move on with our lives, there are so many things we'd trade,
When a song comes on, the words felt deep in our hearts, come right back to us again,
Loving, haunting, joyful and precious, we find it hard to move on within,
I can still hear your voice, your laugh, and see your sweet smile,
But while you're in Heaven, and I'm still here, it never stops hurting all the while,
Until the day we reunite my love, I'll forever have a hole in my heart,
We were together in life, in love, heart and soul, never meant to be apart.

-by Paige

Chapter 3

<u>Emotions, Feelings and Coping</u>

We're All Just Trying to Find Our Way Poem

We're all just trying to find our way,
In a world with so many temptations,
It's so easy to go astray,
But that leads to complications,

We try to be good and get by,
To walk on the straight and narrow,
But wandering off in search of life,
Can shoot you down like an arrow,

When we finally are able to come back up,
We search to find our footing,
But it's hard not to take steps backwards,
The proof is in the pudding,

We're all just human, good deep down,
Trying to make it through each day,
With roadblocks that surface it's all too easy,
To detour and go the wrong way,

We can have it together and then easily slip,
Then want to run away and hide,
None of us are perfect, no matter who,
We're all on this crazy ride,

Courage and strength, that's what we need,
It all sounds easy enough,
Life can throw curves, twists and turns,
The sea can be calm and then rough,

Just take the time to be nice to yourself,
To show yourself love, as you show to others,
Look in from the outside, the box that you're in,
Open the window, breathe the air, break open the shutters,

And tomorrow is always a brand new day,
To start fresh and go the right direction we want,
We have to come to that decision ourselves,
Or inside the feelings of despair will haunt,

We can see clear, and start the right path,
It's never too late when there's a new day,
So be strong and brave, in control as we can,
For we're all just trying to find our way.

-by Paige

We're All Broken Poem

Whether it be me, animals or anyone,
We're all broken, it's true,
No matter where you've been,
No matter where you are, or who,

We all have baggage,
We all get scared,
The nightmares won't stop,
We just need to be prepared,

We've felt and seen things,
For the warning signs are there,
We all have rips and tears,
That need some love and repair,

But until that can happen,
We all need to be aware,
That everyone has problems,
If people judge, it's not fair,

Yes we're all broken,
Inside and out,
We try to get better,
And will with no doubt,

But until then we'll all try,
To be, feel and show our best,
Because that's who we are,
Pure love, above all else.

-by Paige

The Fall Poem

In the fall is when I always seem,
To make the biggest changes,
It's when I feel the clearest,
And able to do some rearranging,

Like the leaves that change their colors,
And become a different hue,
Then gently fall to the ground,
Where the trees can start to renew,

Shedding the old, that's worn with time,
Letting go of the fragile ties,
To become strong again and refresh,
Everything with what in me lies,

I can start again, it's seems easier,
In the crisp, clear, autumn air,
That's when I seem at my readiest,
To become new and repaired,

When I meet special ones,
People and places within,
Can see things more clearly,
And my new life begins,

I guess I'm a tree, or rather we're alike,
That I become renewed in the fall,
I feel my best and can make changes,
That I've needed to start new after all.

-by Paige

Putting up a Wall Poem (about people on/and social media)

I'm putting up a wall,
I have to you see,
There are too many people,
Looking at me,

I need to hide,
Put up my guard,
They're seeing too much,
And it's getting too hard,

I don't want to be too hardened,
And I don't want to become jaded,
But they're hovering is heavy,
To be cynical is something I've hated,

I don't want to see people different,
Or be suspicious of everyone,
But I can't help feeling suffocated,
I just want to run,

Where nobody can find me,
I've put myself out there too much,
I'm tired of people knowing everything,
I want out of their clutch,

It's hurting inside,
One minute they like you, then they don't,
It's weird and it's frightening,
I can't let it get to me, I won't,

But it is making me scared,
And a feeling of being let down,
When they want in my space,
Then suddenly aren't around,

Some I know and some I don't,
There are ones I've never even met,
Any can turn on a dime,
When they don't even know me yet,

They want in, to my secret life,
And I've put it out there to see,
But I'm learning fast many of them,
Are not who they pretend to be,

They act one way, nice and kind,
Whether I know them or not,
Not all of them, mostly ones I don't know,
I let them in too fast, like I forgot,

That I don't know them at all,
These faces they put up to show,
I don't know if they're real or fake,
They show a side, and then they go,

Not really my friends,
Just out in cyberland,
Why does it hurt me?
When they deal a raw hand,

I knew I didn't know them,
So I can't let it get to me,
Only if I truly know people,
As real friends should be,

But even some of those I've found,
Aren't who they say they are,
That's what gets me the most,
When I fall for their false charm,

So whether I know them or not,
I have to protect myself from harm,
Still love all people, but watch more closely,
And have my wall up ready to bear arms.

-by Paige

Just Let Me Be Myself Poem

If I'm not trying to hurt you,
Just please leave me be,
You need to let me find my way,
You don't know what's going on inside of me,

I need my space,
To be who I am,
I'm not doing any harm,
Let me live my life not as a sham,

I'm honest and I'll stay,
That way forever more,
But I need to be myself,
No one slamming me with a door,

I need the door to stay open,
So I know that I'm okay,
To live my life as me,
In my own genuine way,

If you can't accept me,
I'm sorry and I'll hurt deep down,
Because I want you to love me,
No matter what my life revolves around,

Please know I try so hard,
To be the one you want,
I try to meet your expectations,
When I don't all they do is haunt,

But please don't give up on me,
Just let me be myself,
And love me for who I am,
Through sickness and in health.

-by Paige

How Can I Let Someone Treat Me This Way Poem

How can I let someone treat me this way?
They don't have the right,
To make me feel bad about myself,
To the point where I have to fight,

And fighting for what? I know my worth,
Why can't they be fair and see?
Who I am, the person inside,
Who fights everyday just to be,

To be the me, all of us, our true selves,
Why can't people just accept us?
Be nice, real, caring and genuine,
Instead of just trying to judge,

I wish people would be more kind,
To themselves and to others,
Maybe they wouldn't have so much hatred,
If they realized we're all sisters and brothers,

We all have feelings, we all get hurt,
We all feel pain the same way,
So why do we have to watch our backs,
And wonder if we'll become their prey,

It's hard to take, to fathom at times,
How people can be so mean,
They can be so fake, pretend they're nice,
Until you're able to see them come clean,

Without their knowledge, you find out,
Because you're real and good,
The ones to watch for, not to trust,
They're cracks break quick, unlike wood,

Wood is solid, it takes long to weather,
Wood is hard and grounded,
Be like wood, like a strong free tree,
And watch, beware of the woods in which you're surrounded,

Watch for the predators, they're everywhere,
Be sure to watch for stabs in the back,
But know there are only so few of them,
They will eventually crack,

Keep your love and keep your faith,
And always trust your gut,
The rest are good, just like you and me,
The others ones, the cord needs to be cut.

-by Paige

I'll Be Strong Again Poem

How could you leave me?
How could this be?
It was perfect for awhile,
All so wild and free,

Now I have to find,
My own way and mind,
Something I've never done,
I've never been the kind,

That took care of myself,
Emotional or wealth,
In any single way,
I've never known how it felt,

I don't know where to start,
To protect my own heart,
To find my way around,
I've felt like I'm falling apart,

But I will find my way,
No matter what they may say,
I'll make it on my own,
To find a brighter day,

Somehow I'll grow,
How yet I don't know,
But I will survive,
No matter how far I'm thrown,

People may think I'm weak,
I sound strong when I speak,
But I am scared inside,
Though I can't let it leak,

I can be on the outside strong,
I can prove them all wrong,
And be proud of myself,
Like I knew all along,

That though I've never been,
On my own, now and then,
It's shown I have it in me,
And I will be strong again.

-by Paige

Don't Doubt Me Poem

Why do people doubt,
What we're all about,
Who we really are,
Like a shooting star,
Mysterious to some,
But then they just run,
Want to know us inside,
Then leave us and hide,
We showed them our true self,
How we really felt,
We trusted to let them in,
Our circle we keep thin,
Not too many know,
We don't let it show,
The real feelings we save,
Deep and safe in our cave,
But then we let them see,
If we trust them to be,
True to their word,
The words that we've heard,
Have they been honest?
Should we believe they love us?
To keep our secrets,
So we'll have no regrets,
After we let them in,
We hope they are genuine,
To love us as we are,
Don't doubt from afar.

-by Paige

Don't Let People Hurt You Poem

Don't let people hurt you,
They don't have the right,
To try to take your dignity,
To make you have to fight,

Some people don't want to fight,
They just want simple peace,
To be themselves and live,
The life they deserve with ease,

Some will fight back though,
And give you a piece of their mind,
And say words maybe they shouldn't,
Being quiet is hard for them to find,

Either way, it's hard,
When mean people pick on you,
You try to wonder why,
You wonder what to do,

You have to protect yourself,
Do you fight or do you hide?
It's hard to find an answer,
When your world is churning outside,

And inside it can feel deep,
As though you can't even breathe,
What can you do to escape?
To find some beautiful relief,

There are only two ways,
If you run, some call you weak,
Make you feel you can't handle life,
That you're small and that you're meek,

But if you're one to fight back,
Then you can actually look like the bad one,
When you're just defending yourself,
Then they say you should have run,

There's never a right or wrong,
Way to handle the wrongs in life,
You have to be yourself,
And do what you feel is right,

It doesn't matter what anyone thinks,
Trust your gut and your own way,
With that you'll feel you're safe,
Don't let anyone ever take that away.

-by Paige

Jaded Poem

It's hard that it's so easy,
To become so completely jaded,
With no rhyme or reason,
Everything can become so complicated,

When you've been treated unfairly,
And so absolutely unjust,
It's hard to recognize,
Just who you can trust,

People you thought you knew,
You find out just pretended,
You feel stabbed in the back,
Your actions having to be defended,

It's easy to get stuck,
Just to run away and hide,
Away from all of the world,
Just trying to survive,

Everything you knew,
You thought was all correct,
Looking back and forward,
Everyone becomes suspect,

From being able to hurt you,
So nice, then turn to reject,
The heart you hold so dear deep inside,
You must learn to self-protect,

People can turn in an instant,
You think you know them, but don't,
You thought they were sincere,
Letting it happen again, you won't,

Because you can't play this game,
Of being crossed ever again,
You don't know what to expect,
If it will happen, where or when,

So you have to learn and watch,
And listen with an open ear,
That saying about your friends,
And keeping your enemies near,

Is far from the truth you know,
Through your troubles you'll find,
You can't let people harm you,
Or play games with your mind,

Realize who your real friends are,
Keep only those around,
Keep the enemies far away,
Where you can't again be found,

It's sad, but becoming jaded is easy,
Too easy it almost seems,
So protect yourself, learn and grow,
From the bad that life can bring.

-by Paige

Feel Like You're Just Breathing Poem

When you're not home or happy where you are,
Everything's so far apart,
Thoughts and dreams feel really far,

Stealing precious moments from your life,
Wish to see a light in sight,
Trying to let go of lonely fright,

You need to feel to make your way,
Find a path you want to stay,
Where your head can peacefully lay,

You can feel like you're just breathing,
Not living, just being,

A dream that was so far from real,
That you actually can really feel,
It's no longer just surreal,

Deep down in your soul,
A lonely secret goal,
A happiness to hold,

Don't let it go,
You're the only one who knows,
Only you can make it grow,

Don't feel like you're just breathing,
Not living, just being,

Be you,
Be true,
Become new,

No matter where you are,
No matter how far,
It really won't be that hard,

Live your life and be,
And then you will finally see,
You too can be free,

Don't feel like you're just breathing,
You're a living, beautiful being.

-by Paige

I Feel So Depleted Poem

I feel so depleted,
I've totally retreated,
To a safe, happy place,
Where I can find amazing grace,
I can't understand,
How any woman or man,
That you thought was your friend,
Can turn on you in the end,
It's absolutely unfathomable,
To once feel so comfortable,
Around someone you trust,
Then abruptly becomes so unjust,
To tell lies and try to deface,
Put you in a different place,
You have to fight back,
But feel so betrayed by the attack,
It's hard to believe you were friends,
With someone who just pretends,
And gets into your life,
In the end to just cause you strife,
You start to wonder,
What is it that lies under,
These ones you thought you knew,
There seem to be so few,
You let them know your secrets,
And confiding, didn't have regrets,
Until they showed their true selves,
Where meanness actually dwells,
They smile and they act,
Only to stab you in the back,
But as we all are allowed to do,
We can take some time to renew,
Renew our faith in people again,
And hope we can see around the bend,
What lies before us, friend or foe,
But with some people, it's hard to know,
So take time for yourself, to heal,
So we can all recognize who is real,
It's ok to feel depleted when betrayed,
But know that karma will get them some day,
You don't have to be the one that takes revenge,
Just take time, for yourself to mend,
In the long run you'll know that you were better,
Then those people could be, now or ever.

-by Paige

Be Kind to One Another Poem

If you can't be kind,
You might as well be blind,
To the feelings of others,
Like the closing of shutters,
Being cruel is weak,
If someone is, they are bleak,
Everyone has feelings,
Teachings and believings,
If you can't understand,
Move along your own path,
But don't be mean or hurt,
Others on this Earth,
We are all the same,
And different, just as plain,
As day or night,
As wrong or right,
Whatever color we are,
Wherever, near or far,
People are people, all for one,
We all reside, under the sun,
Until the day, we all pass,
And still go the same way at last,
Be kind to one another,
We are all sisters and brothers.

-by Paige

Put All Things into Perspective Poem

I saw a beautiful being today,
Holding their loved ones hand,
While walking through the market,
You see, alone it was hard, for them to stand,

I didn't want to stare,
At that beautiful one, and their face,
With a bandage wrapped around their head,
Where hair once was, it replaced,

Those soft, sweet eyes,
Were outlined thick with black,
Not makeup, or even intended,
But from fighting what's inside, what attacked,

Walking slowly, and with a cane,
Touching not wanted things so delicately,
Items that someone of that age,
For self-care, they shouldn't yet need,

Small in stature, moving slowly,
Any age for that, is young in years,
No one wants to be felt sorry for,
In that moment, I fought back the tears,

My heart filled with love and sadness,
And prayers I started to pray,
For that sweet being I didn't even know,
To get better soon some day,

I wanted to walk by them and smile,
Showing the love I felt and wanted to share,
But they might not know what I meant,
And hurt feelings? No I wouldn't dare,

So I kept my distance, but deep inside,
I was somber and wanted to reach out,
Wanting them to know, there are people,
Who love and care, without a doubt,

They were frail, and yet they were strong,
No matter how they looked,
Making me feel a little guilty,
Of the quicker pace I took,

I've been there before though,
Sick, just not as extreme,
I know how much you realize,
What you had, and again for, you dream,

To be healthy and healed,
And you, whole, once again,
To be the one strong enough,
To lend a helping hand,

Hopefully soon they will though,
Be back to where they once were,
To feeling good, and free from pain,
So much, that the painful past will be a blur,

When I had finally left, and was driving away,
I thought hard, then the tears, they came,
For this one, I could see their beautiful soul,
It showed clearly, not hiding, plain as day,

If that beautiful being that I saw,
Has what, or something, I suspected,
It made me see most problems are really small,
And it put all things into perspective.

-by Paige

(note - this poem I wrote about a beautiful being that was ill that I saw in the market one day, and who struck my heart profoundly)

Reflection Poem

In a world full of hard times,
It's good to sit and reflect,
On changes made and needed,
So we won't have any regrets,

On things that made us happy,
Or things that made us sad,
Challenges to get through,
With things that made us mad,

Getting to a healthy place,
Where we feel alive and free,
From burdens weighing us down,
So we can just live and be,

Be happy and be released,
From guilt or bad places we've been,
Where we got stuck along the way,
But couldn't remember how or when,

To be able to sit and see,
Inside, deep within our souls,
The things we want to change,
And how we can begin to grow,

It's hard sometimes, to relive it,
Remembering the pain,
But if you let yourself get past it,
You'll see sunshine through the rain,

It's the only way to move on,
To stop beating yourself up,
Or letting others walk on you,
To get over it can be tough,

But you have to, you see,
In order to let yourself go,
To a happy, serene place,
Where only you can know,

How good it feels to let go,
Of people or things that hurt,
To let your wings finally show,
And from a caterpillar you convert,

To a fresh new place,
Where nothing and no one is heavy,
You must reflect, forgive and move on,
It's time now, you are ready.

-by Paige

People So Want to be Loved Poem

People so want to be loved,
Like a gift from Heaven above,
Why can't everyone just see,
The beautiful beings we be,
Deep down inside,
Where feelings often hide,
We don't always let it be known,
On our faces even shown,
People can be sweet,
Or seem a little weak,
The can be two-faced,
Those we want to erase,
They can be fake, so look,
Don't let them off the hook,
Let them know you can see,
Who they are, as it be,
Stay away from some,
They'll just make you numb,
Some could hurt you though,
And that you must know,
Steer clear and stay away,
They could take away your next day,
But there are good ones I know,
I've seen them, they show,
Who they are deep down,
Their genuine, solid ground,
Those are the ones you want,
The others they just taunt,
But it is because they were never loved?
They don't know how to give any of,
What they want in return,
To become good and learn,
Maybe some do, maybe some don't,
Trust your gut, so then you won't,
Let them in or near,
Even if you care,
It shows you're the better one,
If your gut tells you run, then run,
But I want to believe,
Everyone is good, to receive,
At least the love they're due,
But it's not up to me and you.

-by Paige

What We Dream Of Poem

What am I doing?
I've fallen astray,
Slowly leaving my normal,
Am I losing my way?

My normal it seems,
Has become quite boring,
It's hard to not see it,
It's too big for ignoring,

Something and someone,
Has slapped me in the face,
It's time to see clearly,
These feelings I can't erase,

I belong to another,
We've been together so long,
But throughout the years,
Some things have gone wrong,

I'm not sure I want it to end,
But a new one has come,
Swept me off my feet,
Trying, but hard, not to succumb,

I don't know what to do,
What if my decision is wrong?
I won't be able to go back,
To what, and who, I knew all along,

The one that I'm with,
Has been so good to me,
And to my loved ones,
We've built a family,

Along the lines though,
And between ups and downs,
We've become so distant,
Still friends, that's all that surrounds,

Boundaries were crossed,
And hard to get over,
Then I find myself,
Finding a new shoulder,

It wasn't what I wanted,
I never searched for another,
But we've become roommates,
Not in love, but still love one another,

It's hard to fathom,
Leaving someone you love,
That I picked and thought,
Would last and be the one,

But love is never certain,
And love is very strange,
How can you love, but not be in love?
How can those feelings change?

It's scary to think of change,
What if I make the wrong decision?
How long do I wait?
So life doesn't become a collision?

I'll wait for awhile,
But should love stay this way?
Or should you move to a new light?
That has maybe come to show you the way,

How do I know?
What's right or what's wrong?
I wish someone would tell me,
Like in the words of a song,

I'm so confused,
And so excited,
I feel like the light in me,
Has been reignited,

But I don't want to hurt anyone,
We still get along,
No fighting or tension,
Just the intimacy is gone,

If someone would just tell me,
What I'm supposed to do,
It would be so easy,
To start something new,

I'll always want him in my life,
I don't want that to change,
So how do I know?
If it's time to rearrange,

Is it supposed to just get comfortable?
It's easygoing, we feel the same,
We're friends, but not lovers,
Is that how it's supposed to remain?

I wish I knew the answer,
And be shown the right road to take,
Because I don't want my decisions,
To cause hurt or be a mistake,

I'll listen with my heart,
And with my mind,
Hopefully what we dream of,
Will be the life that we can all find.

-by Paige

Nothing Left to Say Poem

People say I'm loud,
But I disagree,
It's only because they can't see,
What's going on inside of me,

The fire of passion,
Fighting for what I know is right,
It's only when I become quiet,
I'm letting go of the fight,

I'm wild with my thoughts,
Can go from hot to cold,
I'll try over and over to show you,
How my feelings unfold,

I try to simply love,
Want peace and serenity,
For every living being,
I have so much empathy,

I will try to argue my point,
And have you see why I feel the way I do,
But I can't keep going around in a circle,
When you can't even get a clue,

But if I love you enough,
I'll keep back and forth going,
Only to have you never see,
Or want to hear what I'm knowing,

I know in my heart,
I love you and don't want it to end,
But you start a fight deliberately,
With the words and feelings that you send,

I don't want to say goodbye,
To have any animosity,
It's exhausting though to no end,
When you can't let me feel or talk honestly,

People say I'm loud,
But it's only because I'm trying,
To keep the relationship going,
While it kills me to see it dying,

I don't want to walk away,
We should be able to disagree,
I'm trying to make you see my point,
But we both have to be able to see,

To respect each other's feelings,
Apologize and move on together,
Isn't that one thing love means?
Not be mean or keep the fight going forever,

Forever I wonder about,
Will we be at peace once we've passed?
Will the fighting and misunderstanding be over?
And we can get along at last,

When I've exhausted all resources,
Gone over and over things in my head,
The thoughts running around like wild horses,
Along with the tears that I've shed,

I know that there's still love,
We've been through ups and downs,
No matter how we push and shove,
True love shows it surrounds,

But when there's nothing left to say,
It's hard to keep the will to fight,
Someday we'll make up I pray,
In my prayers every night,

When will the mean words end?
We've shared life, love and laughs,
When will we get along again?
We've made it before through these traps,

We've been through so much,
Supposed to be there for one another,
In each other's lives as friends and a crutch,
No matter what I'll always love you, like no other,

It's only when I'm silent,
No one wins, or has won,
When I have nothing left to say,
That's when I know I'm done,

I don't know how everything turned,
But I know at the end of the day,
It's not when I'm loud you need to be concerned,
It's when I have nothing left to say.

-by Paige

Feeling Betrayed Poem

Feeling betrayed,
My trust for you has gone away,
You were someone,
I thought I could count on,
Someone I looked up to,
I saw a mentor in you,
Told you secrets,
Now I have regrets,
You weren't who I thought,
Or what I want,
In a loving person,
I feel I've been turned on,
You were supposed to be there,
You pretended you cared,
Now I just want to cry,
That space I had for you is dry,
Hopefully my tears will too,
Dry, when I get done missing you,
Because you weren't really "you",
The one I thought I knew,
And you say you don't know me?
That's plain to see,
Because if you really knew me,
And who I am with every heartbeat,
You'd know I won't put up with,
Being so disrupted,
Treated like a stranger,
Now with you, I feel danger,
I'll go my own way,
And know every day,
That I did nothing wrong,
It was you, who all along,
Turned into someone I don't know,
Now a new trusted safe way I'll go.

-by Paige

I'm My Own Person Poem

I'm my own person,
I've known it all along,
I've always been myself,
Even when things went wrong,
I take full credit,
For everything I've done,
It was always my way,
For that prize, I won,
I won at being just myself,
Doing what I needed to do,
In order to become the person I am,
It was the only way that I grew,
I was taught, definitely,
And guided by love,
Whether here on Earth,
Or from Heaven above,
I can only be me,
No one else would I follow,
To be true to myself,
Yesterday, today and tomorrow,
Always be yourself,
No matter what anyone thinks,
If you're not hurting them or you,
Just follow your own true instincts.

-by Paige

I Think You're My Friend Poem

I think that you're my friend,
But,.... then again,
In the world we live in,
It's hard to loyally remain,
Believing what we think,
In a moment, we blink,
Everything can change,
Our lives, rearrange,
From what we thought was real,
From what we see and feel,
Beyond our normal means,
Fantasy turns real it seems,
But then back to reality,
You're you, and I'm me,
Within cyberspace,
It can all be erased.

-by Paige

So in Love with Love Poem

I'm so in love with love,
The kind we all dream of,
Whether it be for myself,
Or for somebody else,
It's such a good feeling to have,
When you feel there's nothing left to grasp,
To be in love with anything,
A human, an animal or anything seen,
Through your loving, wanting eyes,
You'll find it, no surprise,
From the grass, sky or a flower,
In any minute, or any hour,
It belongs inside your heart,
To feel a deeper part,
Of any just regular day,
To find in any way,
The beautiful side of life,
Aside from any strife,
Able to see the beauty and love,
That was sent straight from Heaven above,
Clearly no one here made it,
It's Divine, you can be elated,
Happy and letting it sink in,
No one can take from you that serene,
Feeling that you get and have,
From anything that makes you glad,
To be, and really just "to be",
Helping, without any filters, to see,
Beyond life's seemingly hurdles,
The beauty that lies, and cuddles,
Within your most beautiful dreams,
And in the beauty that brightly gleams,
From any struggles or pain,
Through sunshine and through rain,
When we look as deeply as we can,
From things not made from man,
We can breathe in the beauty and believe,
We were sent that beauty for relief.

-by Paige

I Want to Just Hide Poem

I want to just hide,
I'm tired of the crazy ride,
With people I don't even know,
And nowhere to really go,
Except crazy sometimes it feels,
In a world, where nobody seems real,
Or know each other anymore,
We're just "friends" and "followers",
But not really friends at all,
I don't even know most to call,
If I needed to talk to someone,
To have them over or just to come,
Out somewhere with me,
I don't even know them personally,
To trust who they really are,
We only know each other from afar,
Yet we share details of our lives,
And pictures of our personal times,
But who are we sharing these with?
All of sudden, they can be gone, that's it,
No "see you later" or "goodbye",
No reason or explanation why,
And they know all about us now,
Can pretend to others they know us more somehow,
By having our private pictures saved,
Inside their own personal space,
It's just too weird anymore,
I need to close the door,
To strangers I don't even know,
But have given them my life's show,
And now I see the truth,
It doesn't take a sleuth,
To finally realize,
They're strangers, now I want to just hide.

-by Paige

I'm Gonna be Me Poem

I'm gonna be me,
I'm gonna be free,
Chase my dreams,
See what gleams,
With gold and silver, shiny and new,
Glowing like me in my renewed,
State that I'm now in,
And never leaving, my new beginning,
I have to trust,
And I will, I must,
That I'll be safe and sound,
On lovely solid ground,
That I can walk on and not sink,
Into a shell where I'd have to shrink,
And not be the person that I am,
I'm done with all the pretend,
I'm me and I'm here to stay,
And be me, my own personal way,
And if you don't agree,
Then you don't need to be near me,
Because I only want true people near,
Where the only things that I hear,
Are positive and filled with laughter,
And only happily ever afters.

-by Paige

Chapter 4

<u>Strength, Courage and Healing</u>

Please Don't Doubt Me, I'll Find Me Poem

You take away my pain,
Help me through the strain,
To start another day,

If you doubt me then I know,
I still have more to grow,
More stitches left to sew,

The path to find my way,
Tomorrow's another day,
I never want to stray,

Please don't doubt me,
I'll find me,
I'll make you see,

The me you know that's there,
I'm still here and I'm aware,
Left wide open and bare,

Been so much going through my mind,
For such a long and tortured time,
I still need peace to find,

Please believe me when I say,
I so want another day,
I promise I'll find my way,

No longer filled with fear,
I will be renewed and reappear,
It's your love that helps me dear.

-by Paige

Year of Learning Poem

It's been a year of learning,
Letting go, and for yearning,
Breaking and mending,
Strengthening and bending,
Learning that I can't trust everyone I thought I should,
But learning the ones that I always knew I could,
Learning I have to guard my life and myself,
Putting some feelings up on a shelf,
Where they need to stay, so that I can breathe,
Because thinking about the betrayal, it's hard to find relief,
I can't let it jade me, but I need a wall,
Not too short, but not too tall,
Where if I need to I could jump over or underneath crawl,
Where I could escape without being noticed, away from it all,
Learning is hard, and endless in ways,
From people, to places, we spend all of our days,
It's hard to start it, to really begin,
This caution I need to take and go out on a limb,
Where I can feel safe, quiet and protected,
From the people and things I now feel rejected,
I need to be more private, and close to home,
But never want to lose love and empathy, for ones like I've always known,
I'm learning as I go, and I'll keep writing it down,
So that at some point I can feel I'm strong on solid ground.

-by Paige

Courage Poem

Courage is hard,
It takes a long time,
To find the strength inside,
That behind, you no longer hide,

You have to be raw,
Show your true self,
Let all emotions out,
Put weakness on a shelf,

To find that strong wall,
It's difficult I know,
It's hard not to go backwards,
But it's the only way to grow,

Keeping people and things,
Or being afraid of the unknown,
The things that just bring us down,
That won't let us grow,

It's beyond what you want to do,
You want to rewind and retract,
Once you make that first step,
You have to tell yourself, you can't go back,

It hurts deep inside,
To the depths no one knows,
Could you explain to anyone,
How deep the hurt goes?

Change is so incredibly hard,
Especially when it means possibly the end,
Of the life and love you've been wanting,
It's like no more can you pretend,

That it would be that fantasy,
And that it wouldn't be the way,
You always and ever dreamed of,
That you forever wished it would stay,

The love and life you've always dreamt,
That you've always been craving,
It seems like it's all beautifully happening,
And then all of a sudden it's caving,

You don't want to believe,
It could all go so fast,
The perfect came so quickly,
Then wondering why it couldn't last,

No matter what it is that's hard,
It takes courage and strength,
No matter how anyone acts about it,
Deep down inside it pains,

Even to the strongest ones,
And the ones who show no emotion,
Of course to the ones who show it all,
Inside us, it causes true commotion,

It's hard to let anything go,
It takes so much courage to be brave,
But in the long run we will find,
It's ourselves that we actually save.

-by Paige

Anchor Poem

We all need an anchor,
When we see an anchor we smile,
It reminds us of all things nautical,
It's strong and out in the wild,

The wild sea and ocean that be,
Where nothing can hold you down,
But an anchor actually does,
Just not on solid ground,

The ocean floor is not solid,
It floats and moves around,
It never, ever stays in one place,
It's free, even though it's actual ground,

You feel as if an anchor will hold,
You safe in one place even under water,
But it can actually move with strong force,
And the place you were in, can alter,

To another lovely place,
That's free of all turmoil,
Where fish, mammals and mermaids,
Swim and jump in fun, not set in soil,

They go where they want,
And nothing can hurt them out there,
They can swim away from anything,
Nothing seems untrue or unfair,

And if they can't swim away,
The raging tides are near,
To move them and to save them,
From anything that causes fear,

The huge waves will crush,
And wash away the anger,
So we all can move more freely,
From any eminent danger,

Although danger is everywhere,
In the ocean it seems calm and safe,
From the troubles that we know,
And too often, we must face,

But it seems so surreal out there,
The freedom and Zen we get,
Can't be replaced by anything,
There's nothing of a threat,

And even if there was,
In water, we can get away from it fast,
No danger can stay near us,
Not long will it last,

It doesn't make us stop wanting it,
Especially the sea loving ones,
We love the freedom and groundedness,
An anchor brings and shows,

It's fulfilling our safety we want,
To be stuck, in a safe place,
But is it actually safe where it lands?
This is what we must face,

Maybe it's not in a safe, sacred ground,
Where no one bad can climb aboard,
Like pirates or sea monsters in the night,
Or something that we abhorred,

So it's good that it can move,
On its own or if we pull it up,
We can stay wherever we want,
Or suddenly become abrupt,

The freedom that it brings,
Safe and solid, or free and unfound,
Is what we all dream of and wish for,
That is our own, safe solid ground.

-by Paige

Back to Normal Poem

I want things to get back to normal,
Where there isn't so much turmoil,
I didn't realize what I had,
To have it again, I would be so glad,
We think the grass is always greener,
That we'll have a different demeanor,
If we go somewhere else,
Where we can actually find ourselves,
Then when we get it, what we wanted,
We almost feel as if we're haunted,
Of the life we already had before,
They say one closes, then there's another door,
We look and try to find what it is we crave,
We don't know exactly how to behave,
In a world we wanted, dreamed of constantly,
Can it be, it actually wasn't our cup of tea?
But then when you get it, it's too late,
To change your mind, it's up to fate,
Things happen and change, it's not up to us,
Just go with the flow, it's something we must,
To stay afloat, and move along,
With grace and dignity, we weren't wrong,
To want more, a better life then we thought,
It's what we craved, looked for and sought,
Whether it's what we had wanted, just let go,
Where it can take you, nobody knows,
So when things change, take it in stride,
We're all just here along for the ride,
Enjoy it all, take in everything you can,
Wherever you're meant to be, is where you will land.

-by Paige

The Road to Recovery Poem

The road to recovery is long,
And hard to stay so strong,
When you feel like your world's falling apart,
The stress can be off the charts,
The loneliness can overflow,
Like a feeling you've never known,
You're trying to get to a place,
And sometimes it feels like a race,
That slows down at certain times,
And others times you feel arised,
Then it can go back and forth,
Leaving you feeling of little worth,
You have to take it one day at a time,
Minutes or moments, breathe and find,
That baby steps, are still the only way,
To make it through every single day,
No matter how many times you fall,
Maybe cry, then get up, and face it all,
Changes don't happen just overnight,
Nor did they start that way either, right?
So give yourself a humanly break,
Don't beat yourself up, we all make mistakes,
That's how we learn, that's how we grow,
When we get to that place, we will know,
And be proud of all of our accomplishments,
From all the torments we fought against,
We're all just beings, the same no matter what,
Someday, that tortured door, you will be able to shut.

-by Paige

Going Through Times Poem

Going through times can really bring out the poetry,
Of the feelings I have, deep down inside of me,
A way to express my deepest of thoughts,
To bring me relief, from where I felt caught,
To be able to put it so eloquently,
And give me a feeling of peace and relief,
From burdens or worries, going through my mind,
Where retreating from, can be so hard to find,
To be able to write it, and get it all out,
Is what expression is all about,
Getting things heavy off of your chest,
And finally feeling, and being able, to just rest,
Anything that makes you happy and releases,
The tightness you felt of non-existing leashes,
Is good for your heart, your soul and your mind,
Whatever does that for you, please try to find,
A magical space of your own, no one else knows,
And they never have to, it's only yours,
Try different ways to gently express yourself,
And you'll find something sacred, for you and your health,
No matter what it is, that brings you serenity,
Let that be your secret place, where only you can be,
You can share it or keep it safely tucked away,
And do that special thing, when you need to escape,
The hardships in life, or feelings underneath,
That at times, without this, are so hard to reach,
You'll feel a sense of renewed strength and freedom,
That for you, is your personal, safe magical kingdom.

-by Paige

Heal Your Mind Poem

Sometimes things can seem so hard,
When we get dealt a really bad card,
Nothing seems to flow quite right,
When help seems so far from sight,
No one seems to understand,
It's strange, because they probably can,
But it seems like you're all alone,
And feels like nobody else knows,
The pain that you're going through,
Something strange you never knew,
You don't know quite what to do,
This can't be me, this can't be you,
You fight everything happening inside,
On the outside, you try to hide,
The things that can come out and show,
What's going on, you're about to blow,
It's scary and it's terrifying,
You try, even to yourself, clarifying,
How and what is going on,
How your mind could turn so wrong,
What did this, what do you do?
To get back to the normal you,
Normal that you could at least deal with,
Not this horror that's wanting you to give,
Give up everything, all that you are,
Take it all away, take it so far,
From who you are and what you know,
Where you are and where you go,
You feel crazy, nowhere to turn,
Someone to free you is what you yearn,
But there is help, along our way,
Not many will admit, they feel the same,
If only people would talk about it more,
Maybe we wouldn't feel so scorned,
And helpless with what's going on,
Together, we could feel more strong,
Strong enough to build a bond,
That would help us all to get along,
Along in our own, beautiful lives,
Where we belong and where we thrive,
To know we're not alone at all,
What we're going through, it isn't small,
It's so large, so many know it too,
It's not just me, and it's not just you,
If we stand up and if we speak,
We can find the help we desperately seek,

It's out there, maybe not at first,
But once you ask for help, you've seen the worst,
There are beautiful ways to heal your mind,
If you reach out to many, you will find,
Peace like you've never known,
And the love you've needed, you will be shown.

-by Paige

Be Brave Poem

It's hard to be brave,
In the face of a storm,
Not knowing where to look,
Or who to turn,

Not knowing what's ahead,
Or what awaits,
We have to hold our heads up,
Be strong and face fate,

That can come along,
When we're not ready,
We have to stand our ground,
No matter how heavy,

It seems to be,
Or seems to feel,
Sometimes it seems,
It can't be real,

But reality it is,
So fast, unfortunately,
We have to be ready,
For things we can't foresee,

Have your armor,
On at all times,
Never show fear,
These aren't our crimes,

They are of others,
And we must defend,
Ourselves and our loved ones,
To the absolutely ends,

No one will take us,
Or take us down,
We will fight,
And stand our ground,

So no matter what comes,
Or rears its ugly head,
Be ready, it won't get you,
You'll be the one it dreads,

And when the battle's over,
All said and done,
As long as you stay brave,
No matter the outcome, you won.

-by Paige

Take Me Away Poem

At some point or another,
We all want to be saved,
Sometimes we actually need it,
From the life that we've paved,

When we've made wrong turns,
Not happy with our choices,
It's hard to find a way out,
Alone with just our own voices,

We need strength and guidance,
To help us move along,
To a better place,
To sing a better song,

To feel more at ease,
And more comfortable,
In the new way that we turn,
For the life that we wish for,

But it can be so scary,
To do it on our own,
We want someone to take the reins,
And make our new lives shown,

It would be so easy wouldn't it?
If we can't take that first step,
To move forward by ourselves,
Will it stay the dream we kept?

For so long tucked away,
Deep inside secretly,
But we'll never know,
If we don't, what it could be,

If only we knew, we could always go back,
If it doesn't work out,
But it doesn't always end up that way,
We have to have faith and less doubts,

Until we get to that place inside of us,
Where we're actually able to make the move,
Just keep dreaming and keep hoping,
It's not something we need to prove,

To anyone, to even ourselves,
If it doesn't work out,
But sometimes people are given the push,
And then there's no choice but to shout,

Shout to world, you're ready and will,
Make it on your own, your own way,
But it would be nice just to say to someone,
Take me away, away from all the pain.

-by Paige

Taking Charge of My Life Poem

In this world, I'm becoming skeptical,
In my world, I'm becoming practical,
Some people are not what I thought,
It ended up being a fight that I fought,
With no end in sight,
Till the early morning light,
And even after that,
Still more to spat,
I can't take it anymore,
I have to learn to ignore,
The cruel words that cut,
And bleed my heart and gut,
That echo in my mind,
And hurt every time,
I think of them clearly,
But it's so not healthy,
While trying to forget the pain,
And my own sanity I will regain,
Determined and willing,
This world has become chilling,
So I'm going to take a break,
So as not to make more mistakes,
Trusting way too many people,
That aren't helping me, only cripple,
Now it's time for a lovely change,
In my own way, rearrange,
Taking charge of my life,
And for me, doing what's healthy and right.

-by Paige

When Push Comes to Shove Poem

When push comes to shove,
Look to Heaven above,
It's the only way,
To get through the day,
And through the night,
Filled with secret frights,
That you can't explain,
Sometimes make you insane,
But when you're awake,
These dreams they want to take,
You away from your private world,
All of a sudden you've been hurled,
To a place you didn't know,
And didn't want to go,
But have to it seems,
To change nightmares back to dreams,
When you see that realization,
You try to make the creation,
Of what you would do,
If darkness came to you,
From that deep down place,
You find your sweet escape,
And whether you fight or drift away,
Either way, it's ok.

-by Paige

Don't be Ashamed, to Help the Pain Poem

Don't be ashamed,
To help the pain,
We all go through things,
Life's little rings,
Rings of love,
Or rings that shove,
You into places you never knew,
And in the moment, don't know what to do,
We try, and we try, to do our best,
And keep away from all the rest,
Of the bad, distasteful people around,
Where we feel we're on shaky ground,
We want to get away, hide somehow,
So they can't get to us now,
But it doesn't always work out that way,
So we find ways to not be afraid,
There's many things now in life,
That help with pain, and with strife,
To move along, in your own peaceful way,
And not be led, to a world astray,
Where everything and everyone,
Can drive you crazy some,
To keep peace in your mind,
But don't ever be afraid to find,
Or to ask for some help,
It means more than financial wealth,
You mean more than anything,
To someone, you're their bling,
So don't be afraid, and don't be scared,
To find the ones, who really care,
For help with health, and happiness,
Just let Divine Guidance fix the rest.

-by Paige

Never Lose Your Faith Poem

Never lose your faith,
No matter what it is in you partake,
It can see you through hard times,
When there doesn't seem to be much sunshine,
Things seem cloudy or like a fog,
And we're all just trying to get along,
Through just another day,
We've never been to until today,
We don't know what it'll bring,
Or to whom we can cling,
If we need a hand or shoulder,
Sometimes life gets colder,
Then you ever even imagined,
And it's hard to stay sane,
But if your faith you keep,
Only rewards will you reap,
Because nothing can take that away,
It's yours, to help you along and find your way.

-by Paige

Chapter 5

<u>Inspirational and Uplifting</u>

Give Away the Old, Bring in the New Poem

Give away the old, bring in the new,
Only keep things that mean something to you,
Redecorate, refresh, move them to renew,
Make changes to fit a new improved view.

Things always change and we have to too,
To become more enlightened and to ourselves be true,
So part with the so-so, keep what shows you,
Move things around, it changes the hue.

Find beautiful pieces that can hold more than a few,
Of the treasures no longer out, but still mean something to you,
Never part with those, they're treasures you choose,
One of my absolute favorite things to do.

-by Paige

Keep on Laughing Poem

No matter what is happening,
Laughter is contagious,
Whether something is a little funny,
Or absolutely outrageous,

When you're feeling down,
Laughter can keep you healthy,
It's free medicine for everyone,
If you're not rich, or even if you're wealthy,

It can even help others,
It can make someone's day bright,
To see another human happy,
Can help another see the light,

Even to laugh off your troubles,
It's good in so many ways,
It can turn a day completely around,
And make for better days,

It even feels good to laugh,
Learn to laugh off everything,
Do things that make you happy,
You'll feel the joy it brings,

And if you're treated poorly,
Just remember to laugh it off,
The ones who treat others badly,
Should be the ones laughed at and scoffed,

They can't hurt you inside,
They don't have that power,
So never, ever give it to them,
That power is yours to endower,

So whatever life brings you,
No need to keep grasping,
Letting yourself be happy is the best,
Find the good, and keep on laughing.

-by Paige

There'll be a Brighter Day Poem

How do we grow?
How do we know?
What we can be,
With a future we can't see,
We have to trust,
Have faith, we must,
That it will all work out,
Without a doubt,
We all go through things,
Jump through hoops and rings,
Just to make it through,
It's all we can do,
We're all going to have troubles,
When we want to hide in a bubble,
But everything passes,
Yours is as green as other grasses,
Whether it's good or bad,
No matter what we've had,
Nothing stays the same,
So in your heart, just remain,
Knowing it will get better,
Because nothing lasts forever,
Feel the joy when it's there,
When it's hard, just stay aware,
Stay fearless and strong,
Even if you feel far gone,
Never show fear,
The light WILL appear,
We have to for ourselves,
For our loved ones as well,
For our own well-being, we'll get though,
And find happiness we never knew,
Don't ever give up or give in,
You will be the one that wins,
The world will get better we pray,
For you, there'll be a brighter day.

-by Paige

Smile Poem

It's amazing what a smile can do,
People walk right up to you,
You meet people you never knew,
And they feel drawn to you,

You open yourself up for new doors,
Anything you want can be yours,
Down, around any and all corridors,
Into someone's heart your smile pours,

You could be making someone's day,
From dark and lonely or gray,
Or having the power to change your own way,
To be what you, and others, to God have prayed,

By turning on a light inside,
You can help others and be a guide,
Just like the ocean turns a tide,
And helping yourself with so much pride,

You have no idea where it could lead,
To you or somebody else in need,
Seeing a warm, smiling face indeed,
Can change a heart when it bleeds,

So smile and open yourself and others,
To the lovely call of beckoning colors,
Of being near a soul that beautifully flutters,
Happiness and love, that rids us of all our troubles.

-by Paige

The Bright Side Poem

It's really hard to look on the bright side of things,
When everyone's putting you down,
There are so many people and so much hurt,
When it feels like no one's actually around,

To feel so lonely, in a world so full,
It's a very frightening feeling,
To feel lost with no one to talk too,
All alone, it can send you reeling,

Into a world where you're all alone,
No one seems by your side,
Looking around at so many people,
You're not alone but it's so easy to hide,

The pain you feel, no one else knows,
What you go through day to day,
The struggles of trying to keep it together,
So you don't get lost on your way,

We all need to find, something of our own,
That will guide us toward the light,
The light that accepts us, and won't ever judge,
It will show to us pure and bright,

Don't lose hope, it will come to us,
When we're looking or not, to us all,
Just love yourself and know deep down,
We are just human, but nothing will make us fall.

-by Paige

Don't Ever Let Someone Steal Your Smile Poem

Don't ever let someone steal your smile,
They're not allowed to take it away,
It's yours to keep, and yours to share,
It's good to have your smile every day,

I let someone take mine, foolish of me,
Because they don't have the right,
I allowed them to get to me too much,
It ruined both my day and night,

I can never, ever allow someone,
To do that to me ever again,
I let them take my power that I own,
And realized who is and isn't a friend,

If they're not my friend, they can go away,
Far away from me and my life,
Because I will never give up my power,
It's mine, and they have no right,

I'll hold my smile dear, safe and sound,
I'll keep it on my face,
I'll keep it deep in my heart and soul,
No one is allowed to ever erase,

My smile and happiness, given to me,
We are all given that gift,
And no one can steal it ever again,
It's mine, for me, and to give others a lift,

Life is too precious to let someone hurt you,
And if they try, they're nothing of worth,
For only me and you are allowed,
To have our smiles and the happiness we deserve.

-by Paige

Went to the Chapel Poem

Today I went to the Chapel,
For now it's time to battle,
I know You'll be with me,
What comes I cannot foresee,
But with You by my side,
I don't need to hide,
Your help and Your guidance,
Will carry me in brave highness,
Please hold my hand,
Like no one else can,
And please forewarn,
What lies ahead in the storm,
Please give me the strength,
And courage at length,
To get through the fight,
Let everything be alright,
To fight for my dignity,
For my pride that's within me,
To never let it be taken away,
Please stay and show me the way,
To never show fear,
Of whatever danger is near,
To stand for what I believe,
For I know You won't leave,
To say what's on my mind,
The right words help me find,
I beg You to help hold my stance,
Keep and show my confidence,
I need You to help me through,
To show me what to do,
To help me stand tall,
And no matter what, don't fall,
If I fall for a second,
Your True Grace I beckon,
Please help me back up,
And never give in to the corrupt,
And then please help me to mend,
To never break, only bend,
For then I can rise up again,
And know myself I'm able to defend,
And then when the battle's done,
Please help me know I've won,
Nothing can take me down,
As long as I have You around.

-by Paige

You Mean Something Poem

Whenever you feel shaky and of unworth,
Remember why you put on this Earth,
Because you're beautiful, loving and mean something,
To Divine Guidance and your loving beings,
You're worthy in every sense,
Even just with your presence,
You're a true, rare gem,
Nobody can contend,
There's no one else like you,
That is the magic that you do,
You're original to the core,
Too bad there aren't more,
Just like you out there,
But really, they couldn't compare,
You're genuine and a true gift,
You don't know how much you lift,
The spirits in so many others,
Whether they're happy or have troubles,
They hope that when you're blue,
They can be just as there for you,
So when you're feeling down,
Like no relief can be found,
Remember you mean so much,
To all the lives you touch.

-by Paige

Through the Clouds, So Divine Poem

Through the clouds, so Divine,
The Heavenly rays of sun shine,
They shine upon us, lighting the way,
So we can see the beauty each day,
We tend to miss what's right in front,
Of ourselves, even though it's so blunt,
Everything around us, and everyone,
Has a brightness, that we often shun,
But it's right there, not hidden at all,
What we all seem to be searching for,
The scent of flowers as we walk by,
The clouds creating images in the sky,
The wind blowing past with beautiful ease,
The colors of nature in the leaves,
The smile of someone you don't even know,
When you pass each other on the go,
Saying Hi, just being kind,
Is something in someone, beautiful to find,
The little things in life that bring true joy,
To a day we've never been to, we can be coy,
Not knowing what lies ahead in the day,
While we're all just trying to find our way,
And the beauty we can find in the night,
Looking at stars, so far away, but not from sight,
They shine and twinkle, dance in the sky,
Giving us a beautiful show for awhile,
And let us know how little we actually are,
In a world and universe so close and so far,
If we think sweet thoughts, look for the good,
Hopefully we can see life the way that we should,
With beauty from our hearts, our souls and our eyes,
We'll find that everywhere, Divine beauty lies.

-by Paige

Be Happy for the Little Things Poem

No matter what life brings,
Be happy for the little things,
Like the bird outside that sings,
And maybe it's almost spring,

The dew upon the leaves,
The sweet smell of the breeze,
The closeness of a squeeze,
When a hug's so tight you can barely breathe,

The chimes that sway in the wind,
When their soft lullabies begin,
You want to take it all in,
And be swept away by their Zen,

The colors of a magnificent sunrise,
Can leave you with a feel of surprise,
That you're finally able to realize,
It's like something you've only fantasized,

The beauty that's surreal,
To any way you feel,
Little things can have so much appeal,
You know that pure loveliness is real,

Looking deeply you recognize,
That within all things true beauty lies,
Nature in all its glory arise,
And you can breathe relieving sighs,

Of knowing the sun will set each night,
No matter if things are wrong or right,
The stars will burst out with delight,
And joy to lighten all of our fright,

For it's the little things that matter as a cure all,
In a day, in your life, and at all,
No matter how big or how small,
They are the things we remember by far,

So when things get too big to handle,
Enjoy the flickering of a subtle candle,
Appreciate the seasons, and then you will,
Be able to be happy from every angle.

-by Paige

Tomorrow Poem

No matter what you're going through,
Yesterday or today,
We all have the chance,
To start a new day,

Tomorrow when you wake,
The sun will rise again,
Even if there are clouds,
It's a new day to begin,

Begin again to what,
And who you want to be,
It's never too late,
For any of us to see,

To try again,
No matter how much,
We need in able to be,
Where we feel in touch,

With our hearts and our minds,
It doesn't matter how many,
Times that we need,
Until we are ready,

To start a new way,
The life that we dream,
It's not far away,
Even if it seems,

Because tomorrow is always,
Another chance,
To better yourself,
To start a new dance,

No one can tell you,
When it should happen,
It will when it's time,
For our lives, there's no mapping,

Because no matter where you've been,
Or what you're going through,
Tomorrow's a new day,
Every day we can start new,

So go to sleep,
And all tears, you wipe,
Because tomorrow's the first day,
Of the rest of your life.

-by Paige

Everyone Needs a Hand Poem

Life can be so hard,
A lot of ups and downs,
Which way do you go?
So many turnarounds,

Trying to choose,
The right and safe path,
Difficult decisions,
To escape any wrath,

Which way is right?
None of us know,
Which way is wrong?
Which way do we go?

Until we get there,
It's hard on our own,
To know the next step,
We're not exactly shown,

We have to really think,
And we have to guess,
Will it be the right choice?
To work out for the best?

If we're alone it's even harder,
That burden to bare,
When we don't have anyone,
With which to share,

To help us to move,
In the right directions,
Where we're hopefully faced,
With less than more rejections,

In such a big world,
No matter how strong one seems,
We all need others, or just one,
To help us reach our dreams,

We all need someone to trust,
That we can always turn to,
No matter what the issue,
They're always there for you,

Whatever anyone says,
They don't really want to be alone,
No matter what the love is,
A true love is pure gold,

Whether it is a couple in love,
Or your beloved dear family,
It can be a close friendship,
Doesn't matter, it's yours, the key,

The key to open any doors,
You don't want to walk through alone,
They're always there, by your side,
Their loyalty, and yours is known,

It's never wavering,
Or a guessing game,
So close that even during fallouts,
They're over fast, you're back to the same,

So look the world over,
And find these special ones,
They may be right in front of you,
Or somewhere else under the same sun,

Keep looking around, and try to find them,
They're looking for you too,
And never, ever give up,
You'll find each other soon,

We all need a hand,
Every single day,
Whether it's to help you up,
Or to hold along the way.

-by Paige

Our Calling Poem

How do we hear our calling?
How do we know?
Listen to the wind, nature, how you feel,
That's the only way we'll grow,

Always searching,
Can't seem to find,
What it is I was meant for,
My destiny that's mine,

I want it so much,
The motivation is there,
But there are so many things,
I'm not yet aware,

What I was meant to do,
In this big, wild world,
What my calling is,
I haven't quite heard,

Someone please tell me,
I beg and I plead,
It's something I wish for,
Something I need,

We all need something new,
Something's are a given,
Like raising a family,
Or finding a road less driven,

Time passes and we see,
That families grow their own way,
We don't let them go,
They stay near we all pray,

So we need to find,
What else is meant for us,
Alone, deep inside,
That can make us feel just,

Just the way we need,
At certain times in our lives,
We need them to feel,
To grow and to thrive,

It doesn't take away,
Anything else we have,
It's just something we can give,
And something we can be glad,

And proud to share,
Fill any emptiness we felt,
To feel needed again,
That once started to melt,

The yearnings we have,
All of us feel,
We'll find the way to fulfill them,
And make a new calling real.

-by Paige

Find Happiness Poem

Try to find happiness,
With the littlest of things,
It's amazing when you look,
At all that life brings,

There's so much anger,
And so much dismay,
Things mean and unkind,
Just going from day to day,

But if we really look deeply,
And search inside of ourselves,
We're able to see the beauty,
And overlook the dwells,

Just smiling to oneself,
Having a smile upon your face,
Can take you to a different level,
And to a much higher place,

Where no negativity,
Can get through to you,
No bad energy,
Will leave you feeling due,

You'll brighten deep inside,
And your light will show through,
It will lift up your spirits,
And lighten your mood,

So whatever is thrown your way,
Take a deep breath,
Focus on happiness,
And it will do the rest.

-by Paige

True Love Will Find its Way Poem

When I think of the heartache,
That life can throw around,
It saddens me to think,
It's hard to find safe ground,

So much discomfort,
So many out there fake,
Nowadays even more,
It's easy to mistake,

People and things,
All around us, or behind a web,
It's hard to see clearly,
Or can become something we dread,

To know what is real,
And who's real that we can trust,
We want to be kind,
But self-protect we must,

Everyone's looking,
Looking for love and happiness,
Why is it so hard to find?
Why can't we have it like the rest?

It seems like they do,
But actually so many are the same,
Trying to find a way out,
Of the unknown web of games,

So don't let yourself get caught,
Inside of a wicked lair,
Where boundaries get crossed,
And love was never really there,

Be smart and be safe,
Be true to your heart and stay,
Have patience, when the time is right,
For you, true love will find its way.

-by Paige

I'm in Love with My Life, Because it's Mine Poem

I'm in love with my life,
Because it's mine,
No matter how shattered,
No matter how fine,

We only get one,
And I have no regrets,
For everything I've done,
Has been kismet,

I've made it though,
The good times and the hard,
Sometimes it wasn't easy,
But sometimes not marred,

It's made me who I am,
And I won't say sorry,
Because I love who I've become,
It's actually quite cathartic,

To be able to express myself,
In all of my years,
May have brought happiness,
May have brought tears,

But it did do something,
It brought me to me,
To who I really am,
And to who I'm supposed to be,

Not fake, not phony,
It's only me and real,
I'm who I am, take it or leave it,
That's me, genuine, it's how I feel,

My love will never change,
My soul will stay the same,
My feelings will never stray,
My heart will, forever remain.

-by Paige

Be in Love with What Makes You Happy Poem

Be in love,
With what makes you happy,
No matter the cost,
No matter how sappy,

It will mean something to you,
And to the ones you love,
By bringing so much happiness,
To everyone engulfed,

In your love and your circle,
The ones that you know,
You can always count on,
And them on you as though,

There isn't any other,
As just quite the same,
As you and your loves,
Quite sacred they'll remain,

Whoever it is,
Or whatever it may be,
It's yours alone to love,
And devour it with glee,

No one can take,
That away from you or me,
For all of our lives,
We will be, who we will be,

Embrace it, embrace you,
Embrace you and me,
For the genuine are strong,
And forever we will be free.

-by Paige

Take Me Ocean, I'm Yours Poem

Take me ocean, I'm yours,
I could stay with you all day and night,
Your sound, smell and feel, I adore,
No matter what, you always feel right,

Your colors surround me,
And I surround myself with your colors,
Giving me a sanctuary,
And home feeling like no others,

You make me feel peace,
I could sit and look at you all day,
You change and are never the same,
Yet beautiful in every way,

How can you be so peaceful?
Yet so fierce at the same time?
You beauty is like no other,
Distilling Zen in my mind,

Your salty smell is fresh and cleansing,
Your breeze is unwavering and feels free,
Your sound of mounting, crashing, then calm,
Slowly flowing back to the sea,

You clear my mind,
You cleanse my soul,
Your sands are massaging,
Whether they're warm or they're cold,

I want to be with you forever,
Never leave your tide,
Play in the ocean and sands,
All along you far and wide,

Through everything I've tried,
Nothing makes me feel as calm as you do,
I don't know what it is,
The mystical magic of you,

When I'm near you I can't wait to see you,
When I'm with you I don't want to leave,
You give me such calm serenity,
You're healing is to be believed,

I feel better when I'm with you,
I dream of you being near,
You make me feel more like me,
You're home, you drown my fears,

Nothing scares me when I'm near to you,
Nothing can hurt me, just heal,
It's lovely how you spread your vitamin sea,
It's indescribable how you make me feel,

I always knew I loved you,
I was with you all the time,
But I didn't realize until I left,
How freeing you made my mind,

To swim in your waters, free and open,
You help me find my footing to walk in your wet sand,
I feel grounded, able to hold my stance,
You're the only place I feel stable on land,

I hope that when my time here is over,
My body can be spread into you forever,
And be able to feel the freedom and Zen,
That you have given me in life, my favorite pleasure.

-by Paige

(note – this a poem I wrote about myself standing in the ocean's waves coming up onto the beach, enveloping me in their serenity, it's the cover picture on my book)

A Lovely New Start Poem

A lovely new start,
A brand new year,
To lift my heart,
And get rid of fear,

To glow inside and out,
Like I've wanted to for so long,
My new leaves will sprout,
And bad habits will be gone,

A time to grow,
To begin a new change,
It's never too late you know,
To, in many ways, rearrange,

Baby steps, or outright,
Either and any way I want,
I'll have peace and not lose sight,
Of the way I wish to be from now on,

I've been wanting to start fresh,
But it takes time you know,
To want and finally address,
That I'm ready, heart and soul,

I'll stay strong and feel peace,
Not wavering from my goals,
So many things to seize,
So many new to take hold,

I won't let myself down,
Or anyone else for that matter,
I want this truly crowned,
And not let anything shatter,

My new ways I've craved,
For so long now it seems,
My healthy life road paved,
I can see the way, new light beams.

-by Paige

Confidence Poem

Show your confidence and stand tall,
Even when you're feeling small,
It will change how you feel about things,
And you'll see and feel the change that it brings,
Not only will you see yourself in a new light,
Everyone else will see your light shine bright,
It will shine as you walk, stand and just be,
Like a lighthouse guiding the ships at sea,
You'll feel it more, deep down inside,
No longer wanting or able to hide,
You're newfound confidence will now grow,
And you, and the world, will see and feel your glow.

-by Paige

A Special Place Poem

In this big wide world,
You need to find a special place,
Where no one can hurt you,
Where you feel serene and safe,

No matter where it is,
It's all up to you,
To retreat and find refuge,
When you need solace or feel blue,

To have peacefulness and quiet,
No one else is allowed,
To invade your secret space,
That would be a crowd,

Whether it be some certain place,
Or alone in your head,
Some imaginary dream,
Even tucked safe in your bed,

We all need an escape,
No matter where or what it may be,
Never be ashamed,
Of where you find your serenity,

It's your place, wherever you want,
To wash some things away,
We all need comfort and solitude,
To be ourselves, no need to explain.

-by Paige

Every Day is a Fresh Start Poem

I can't be sorry for who I am,
I am me for a reason,
I can't change, but I can try,
To be the best I can at pleasing,

To please the ones I love the most,
But still be true to myself,
Please accept who I am,
Everyone is full of wealth,

Maybe not the material kind,
Or full of money or gold,
But I'll show you the real, that I am,
From my youth until I am old,

Please don't judge me at all,
It will be me, and I will be real,
The genuine one you know,
The one that you can feel,

When you doubt me,
Or feel that I'm lost on my path,
Please know I'm not perfect,
I'll find my way back,

A moment a weakness,
Does not a person make,
We are allowed to learn,
Even if we continue our mistakes,

I'm human as we all are,
No matter my age, I do my best,
When we're young we want to be older,
To fit in with the rest,

But as we get older,
Harder times actually become,
We wish we could go so far back,
We see how easy it was when we were young,

We could hide, or maybe not,
But we had ones to hide behind,
That never left us or let us down,
No matter what was on our mind,

Maybe someday we can all be perfect,
But what is perfect in reality?
No one is, that's why we need,
To accept each other in totality,

Please just love me, as I am,
And don't judge me along my way,
And know I'll try as hard as I can,
To be the one you want and say,

To say to others who I am,
And know deep in your heart,
That I'm still me, no matter what,
Every day is a fresh start.

-by Paige

Angels Poem

I believe that Angels,
Are always with us and around,
Around us whether we can see,
Or feel them, or hear a sound,

They are hovering around us,
And protecting us at all times,
Whether we can find them,
They're there, quiet as mimes,

Guiding us along the way,
Or sitting with us through pain,
They are with us, constantly,
Through our sunshine and our rain,

Although we don't notice,
They speak into our ears,
The Heavenly words they say,
Ring in, and we hear,

What is best for us,
And what we need to do,
The Angel on our shoulder,
Is definite and true,

Always listen with your soul,
With your mind and with your heart,
You'll know when you're hearing them,
Every moment they're a part,

Of us and of our lives,
Nothing can come between,
The love of the Heavenly Angels,
That come to intervene,

Intervene us from the bad,
And from the negative,
From the evil in the world,
And save us from the wicked,

They do actually show themselves,
But only in near death,
Whether we live or we die,
They show their actual depth,

When they do know it's time,
And the Angels do appear,
To see them is beyond anything,
They're more REAL than anything real,

You see and feel them with your soul,
It's so calm, you just feel love,
You're not scared, you don't feel alone,
Just the opposite, they're from Heaven above,

From above the tapestry of life,
The beauty we don't even know,
We only see the underside,
The messiness and knots, in no real row,

But once they show themselves,
There's a beauty you've never known,
That is so capable and strong,
The first time you ever see a true glow,

They are amazing to see,
Amazing to feel,
Just like you thought,
They protect you for real,

They're sweet, and they're strong,
Angels are fierce warriors,
They're Messengers of God,
And help us to be forewarned,

They hold you and comfort you,
When no one else is around,
No matter when or where,
Our Angels can always be found,

Never doubt that they are there,
Whether they show themselves or not,
We're never alone with our Angels,
Just talk to them, they listen more than we thought.

-by Paige

Zen, Now and Always Poem

I so do love you,
I love your wild spirit,
I love how you're untamed,
And totally fearless,

You walk your own walk,
And dance in the rain,
You howl at the moon,
See sunshine where there's pain,

March to the beat of your own drum,
It doesn't matter who's around,
When you're around nature,
Beauty can always be found,

I admire your courage,
Your independent streak,
You're strong and you're stubborn,
Not caring what others think,

Your heart is made of gold,
You're kind, gracious and sweet,
Empathetic to all,
No matter who you meet,

You're genuine and true,
Definitely one of a kind,
With your own way of doing things,
Once you've made up your mind,

And when you make decisions,
Nothing can change how you feel,
But it all comes from a happy place,
You love, are the real deal,

Never change for anyone,
You wouldn't, not a chance,
You're a take me or leave me kind,
Not giving a second glance,

People like you are rare,
You say what you feel inside,
No pretension or pretending,
You're feelings, you can't hide,

You're free from inhibitions,
Reckless, fierce and fun,
No standing in your way,
You need to be wild to run,

So those are just a few of the things,
I love that you'll forever stay,
You gentle, beautiful, free being,
I love you, Zen, now and always.

-by Paige

You're Something to Someone Poem

We all can feel doubtful,
On any certain day,
We can feel so unneeded,
In every possible way,

But the fact of reality,
Is we are all needed so,
By people we're close to,
Or we might not even know,

People can have a hard time,
Putting into words,
The feelings that they have,
And then they go unheard,

When they're so badly needed,
And wished upon to hear,
To know we mean something,
That to someone, we are dear,

When feelings are kept secret,
It's a shame and tragedy,
For who knows who needs them,
A little saving it just might be,

To one in need of love,
Of acceptance and of peace,
Wanting and yearning,
To put our minds at ease,

Knowing we make somebody,
Feel happy and safe,
Comfortable and cozy,
By something we radiate,

We're able to give out,
This positive energy,
It might be something seen,
Or something no one can see,

But with this love and feel,
We're able to create,
A peaceful feeling for someone,
It's called their safe place,

So when you're feeling low,
Like you don't even matter,
Know there's always someone,
That without you, life would shatter,

No matter who you are in life,
No matter what you've got,
You're something to someone,
Whether you know it or not.

-by Paige

Let People Be Poem

Let people be,
Who they are, what they are,
No matter how close,
No matter how far,

We're all going through something,
At some point in our lives,
It's how we get through,
It's how we survive,

That shows our strength,
That tells our tale,
Of how we make it through,
Of how we prevail,

Why can't people,
Be accepted as they are?
We all matter differently,
And the same by far,

We are all unique,
And work in different ways,
Whether we are like nights,
Or whether we are like days,

No one is the same,
And that's perfectly ok,
Because our differences make us,
Unique in our own ways,

Try not to judge,
When people aren't the same,
As you or someone else,
Because all human, we remain,

And once people see,
And start to realize,
We're all the same, but different,
It opens people's eyes,

To our differences we have,
And to how we are real,
We all have opinions,
But in the end, we all feel,

So let people live,
And let people be,
We'll all be ok,
When we're ready, we'll see.

-by Paige

Be Nice Poem

Be nice to people,
We're all not the same,
In ways we are,
But we're not to blame,

We can be different,
Others don't understand,
What we're going through,
It's not what we planned,

Life is different,
And difficult for some,
Some don't seem to get it,
It's hard to overcome,

But tough love doesn't help,
Understanding and acceptance do,
People need to realize,
They're just like me and you,

No matter how perfect,
Someone's life seems,
It might be not perfect,
Falling apart at the seams,

But can the seamstress help?
And sew it back together?
Despite the hardships,
And the stormy weather,

It's difficult to imagine,
That one really could,
But it would be so lovely,
If they really would,

But until that happens,
Until we're all perfect,
Which we'll never be,
Be nice, everyone will profit.

-by Paige

Embrace Change Poem

I know it's hard,
Life's many changes,
Out of our comfort zone,
Nothing seems stranger,

But it's always inevitable,
That life will change lanes,
And we have to keep going,
Through the sunshine and the rain,

Changes can be scary,
And hard to get through,
Or they can be a blessing,
We needed but never knew,

The only way though,
To move on and still go,
On with our lives,
Is to roll with the flow,

Where it takes us,
We don't know,
It would be nice to see ahead,
But we will learn and we will grow,

Somehow, someway,
Even if we don't know the next step,
We have to take it,
Go forward, but always protect,

You, and your loved ones,
Inside and out,
After all, that's life,
And change is without a doubt,

One of our biggest hurdles,
And what a lot of life's about,
It's normal to be scared,
To want to cry and shout,

But trying to accept things,
Can be easier said than done,
But being able to embrace change,
Will help in us all in the long run.

-by Paige

In Love with Life Poem

I'm so happy right now,
So in love with life,
So many ups and downs,
So much good, yet through strife,

It's amazing how everything,
Can change in a heartbeat,
One day it seems hard,
The next, all ends meet,

And can come together,
Like you never dreamed,
From falling apart,
Everything at the seams,

And then like magic,
If you roll with the flow,
Everything falls into place,
The way it's supposed to roll,

None of us know the future,
Or exactly what's right to do,
But if you let Divine Guidance work,
It's amazing how It guides you,

Don't over think things,
Don't read too much into life,
We're going to go on our own path,
And it will all work out right,

The way it's supposed too,
With all the forks in the road,
But if we just ask for guidance,
Our way will be shown,

Love the beautiful moments,
And try not to worry too much,
Believe what's in your heart and soul,
Then true love will never leave your touch.

-by Paige

Love and Harmony Poem

Peace and serenity,
Sweep over me,
Like a dance of the ocean,
Casting calm like the sea,

I swift and I sway,
To the peaceful song,
Of the waves dancing,
Like they have all along,

They take me away,
From the world that we know,
Where hate and silence,
Too often grow,

I drift and I dream,
Of places far oft,
Where silence and love,
Aren't only just thought of,

Where everything belongs,
And everyone can be,
In solitude and strength,
With love and harmony.

-by Paige

The Ocean Poem

If we could all just sit by the water,
And let our cares just drift away,
What a wonderful world we might live in,
Where peace and love are simply day to day,

Where letting go of your worries,
Is as easily done as said,
Just pour yourself into the ocean,
And let go of what's in your head,

Let the waves envelope you,
Use its cleansing power,
Let them wash your cares away,
It's there for you to devour,

You'll feel it lighten your load,
Let everything slip away,
The freedom of the ocean,
Puts you at ease in a way,

A way that nothing else can,
It has a way to release,
The pain and complications,
That from, can be so hard to find relief,

In life we all have difficulties,
But the ocean is a gift,
Given so sweetly by God,
To give our spirits a lift.

-by Paige

The Bay Poem

The bay is calm, with islands all around,
You can sit in silence, and not hear a sound,
Of the world outside, that from within, you hide,
The peaceful little beaches, that shelter you with the tide,
No rough pounding here, just peaceful, gentle waves,
You can't help but feel, the easiness each gave,
That sway up loosely, calm and so close,
Just sit, and be, that's where you find, what you feel and need the most.

-by Paige

The Beach and Ocean Poem

The moment you arrive,
The smell of salt in the air,
You feel more alive,
Without even a care,

When you step on the sand,
That first melting in,
To the warm, soft grains,
And the feeling on your skin,

You feel the ocean breeze,
Blowing all around,
It puts you at ease,
Like you're no longer on the ground,

You feel open, happy and alive,
Wildly loose and free,
Feeling that ocean vibe,
Calm and serene, you can just be,

Everyone is themselves,
Lets loose and no worries,
Problems are put on a shelf,
At the beach, you're in no hurry,

As you walk closer near,
There you see the ocean,
The serenity appears,
Like a secret love potion,

It's captivating and mystical,
Losing yourself in its waves,
The sounds are soothing and whimsical,
You could be lost in it for days,

You can just sit and be,
And think about nothing,
Or retreat inside your being,
And deeply think of everything,

If the water calls to you,
You have to step in,
For its calling you true,
To feel what lies within,

Right when you're there,
You can feel it so well,
If something had you scared,
It's washed away in a swell,

To be swept by the waves,
Circling around your feet,
The foams cleansing haze,
You feel so complete,

When the waves crash around,
You can feel off balance,
Instead you hear their calming sound,
And do a little dance,

The waves sweep back out soon,
Leaving your footprints in the sand,
Then rush back in to grab you,
You find your footing in the land,

The ocean is strong and wild,
But what you soon find out,
Is that the same as a child,
You have no fear or doubt,

You could stay here forever,
Just watching it, you're mesmerized,
You and the ocean together,
Are beautifully etherealized.

-by Paige

The Beauty of Nature Poem

The beauty of nature,
Of feeling serene,
Keeping away meanness,
Able to thrive through the foreign,

It succeeds like you wish,
You could only do,
To survive the elements,
If you only knew,

Things that surround us,
We clearly so fight,
With intentions of good,
We have clearly a right,

Presence of love,
Seen so clear,
We hardly need,
To see far or near,

The beauty of ease,
The serene so nice,
There's no emptiness,
Only sweet spice,

The breeze of purity,
Is so real and so far-fetched,
In this world we feel,
It's just in pictures, just etched,

But it can be real,
What's felt in our hearts and souls,
Being able to survive,
No matter what unfolds,

I wish and I pray,
That we all can see,
All along the way,
That we all can succeed,

Whether we're watered a lot,
Or left, just a little while,
We strengthen while alive,
We will survive, no denial.

-by Paige

The Rain Poem

I love how the rain,
Washes everything clean,
It can take away pain,
And feel so serene,

On a cloudy day,
When the sprinkles start to come,
It's so comfy just to lay,
In your bed at home,

Cozy under the covers,
Where you're able to hide,
Away from any others,
Like no other way you've tried,

You can also stand in the rain,
And cry if you want,
To get rid of the pain,
That's been hurting your heart,

No one will know at all,
They'll blend with your tears,
The raindrops that fall,
With feelings built over years,

Or you can be happy and smile,
Looking up at the sky,
Knowing all the while,
Your loved ones are only a mile,

If even that far away,
They're showing us they're near,
As if they're trying to say,
They also cry, with Heavens tears,

No matter what we're feeling,
The drops are cleansing and Zen,
Anything that's been reeling,
Is washed away, a has-been,

And with the smell of the Earth,
After all of the rain,
It's called petrichor I learned,
So lovely, it takes your breath away.

-by Paige

Thank you so much for reading! I hope you like them as much as I love them! If any of my poems touched or helped anyone in any way, that makes me happy! Peace and love to everyone!

www.ingramcontent.com/pod-product-compliance
Lightning Source LLC
LaVergne TN
LVHW041320080426
835513LV00008B/528